C++ Networking 101

Second Edition

Build strong expertise into programming sockets, protocols, VPNs, and asynchronous I/O with 75+ sample programs

Anais Sutherland

Published by: GitforGits

Publisher: Sonal Dhandre

www.gitforgits.com

Printed in India

First Printing: November 2024

ISBN: 978-81-974165-4-5

Cover Design by: Kitten Publishing

Disclaimer:

This book, including all its text, diagrams, and illustrations, is an original work developed for educational and informational purposes. The content is not affiliated with, endorsed by, or sponsored by any company, brand, or entity referenced within. All brand names, product names, and trademarks mentioned are the property of their respective owners and are used in a descriptive, educational context only. Every effort has been made to ensure that no copyrighted or trademarked material has been copied or misused in this book. All diagrams and illustrations that are not original have been used with proper attribution and credit to their respective sources.

If you believe that any content in this book infringes upon your copyright or trademark, please contact us immediately at support@gitforgits.com. Upon notification, corrective action will be taken promptly.

Prologue

With the first edition of C++ Networking 101, I tried to help C++ programmers connect the dots between the language's basics and practical networking. The response was way more encouraging than I ever expected. Folks from all over the world reached out to me, telling me how they built their first TCP clients, configured real routers, or automated tasks using the examples in the book. Plenty of folks said it was how they got their start in network programming and administration. That kind of feedback made all the long nights of writing and coding worthwhile. They also gave some great editorial suggestions. Some folks were hoping for more technical detail in certain areas, especially around asynchronous programming, protocol implementation, and real device configuration. And others wanted smoother transitions between conceptual explanations and practical examples. Some folks mentioned that while the first edition covered a lot of topics, a few sections relied too much on theory without giving them enough hands-on structure. I listened closely to these voices. This second edition is my response to them.

In this new edition, I've been working on making the teaching flow better and making the technical stuff clearer without overwhelming you. I wanted every chapter to feel like a conversation between us—structured, progressive, and engaging. First, you'll get the basics down, like how C++ works well with TCP/IP and how sockets are the foundation for communication. Then, I'll show you how to build real client-server apps, set up IP addressing, and use protocols like HTTP, FTP, SMTP, IMAP, and DNS directly through C++ code. Each example is practical and you can actually implement it. It shows you not just how something works, but why it matters in real networking scenarios.

As you move forward, the book shifts gears into the operational world. You'll be automating device configurations using NETCONF, managing firmware updates securely, tuning TCP and UDP settings for performance, and recovering devices during failure events. You'll also get to work with asynchronous programming, multithreading, and network simulation tools, and you'll build confidence as you gradually work your way up to more complex tasks. It's got some really exciting stuff, like a chapter on monitoring, in which I'll walk you through integrating Nagios with your network and extending its checks using custom C++ programs. You can automate things like fault detection, performance tracking, and security oversight. This edition is designed to make the learning experience both structured and engaging. You'll see the code, run it, see how it works, and gradually get better at it. I've kept the examples accessible so that even if you're not an advanced programmer, you can follow along and succeed. At the same time, the content has enough technical depth to give experienced readers valuable insights.

This isn't a book to put on a shelf. It's meant to be used, tested, and adapted as you build your networking skills. I'm excited to join you on this journey.

Content

Preface

The point of this edition is to help C++ programmers get the skills and confidence they need to do a wide range of networking tasks. The book gives lots of practical, easy-to-follow examples and covers most key areas of network programming, but intentionally leaves out highly complex scenarios. It starts with the basics of how C++ works with TCP/IP and gradually builds on that as you learn to write client-server applications, configure IP addressing and subnets, implement protocols like HTTP, FTP, SMTP, IMAP, and DNS, and handle network communication errors effectively. It's packed with clear explanations and real code that works.

You'll dive into VPN setups, wireless networking standards, asynchronous programming models, and network simulations, using modern C++23 features throughout. As the chapters go on, the focus moves on to getting the most out of devices and making them run smoothly. This includes using NETCONF to automate device configurations, managing firmware updates, tweaking socket behavior for better performance, setting up recovery systems, and making diagnostic tools. You'll also set up network monitoring using Nagios, along with custom C++ checks to track faults, performance metrics, and security events in real time.

After finishing, you'll be able to think and work like a network programmer and administrator, and you'll be ready to use your skills in real-world situations.

In this book you will learn how to:

- Build strong foundations in TCP/IP networking using modern C++ coding examples.
- Work on client-server applications with TCP and UDP sockets, and get to know real-world communication patterns.
- Get hands-on with IP addressing, subnets, and routing through practical demonstrations and progressive programming exercises.
- Put core application protocols like HTTP, FTP, SMTP, IMAP, and DNS in C++.
- Take advantage of NETCONF and C++ to automate configuration tasks across network devices efficiently and consistently.
- Employ asynchronous programming, multithreading, and event-driven models to handle high-performance networking scenarios.
- Program your devices to automatically update their firmware, adjust their settings, and recover if something goes wrong.
- Combine Nagios monitoring with custom C++ checks for fault, performance, and security visibility.
- Simulate and test networks using NS-3 and diagnostic tools for real-time problem solving.

GitforGits

Prerequisites

This book **"C++ Networking 101, Second Edition"** is designed for programmers who know the basics of C++ and want to confidently enter the world of network programming and administration. This hands-on book bridges the gap between programming fundamentals and practical networking tasks, enabling you to build real, working systems step by step.

Codes Usage

Are you in need of some helpful code examples to assist you in your programming and documentation? Look no further! Our book offers a wealth of supplemental material, including code examples and exercises.

Not only is this book here to aid you in getting your job done, but you have our permission to use the example code in your programs and documentation. However, please note that if you are reproducing a significant portion of the code, we do require you to contact us for permission.

But don't worry, using several chunks of code from this book in your program or answering a question by citing our book and quoting example code does not require permission. But if you do choose to give credit, an attribution typically includes the title, author, publisher, and ISBN. For example, "C++ Networking 101, Second Edition by Anais Sutherland".

If you are unsure whether your intended use of the code examples falls under fair use or the permissions outlined above, please do not hesitate to reach out to us at support@gitforgits.com.

We are happy to assist and clarify any concerns.

Acknowledgement

I owe a tremendous debt of gratitude to GitforGits, for their unflagging enthusiasm and wise counsel throughout the entire process of writing this book. Their knowledge and careful editing helped make sure the piece was useful for people of all reading levels and comprehension skills. In addition, I'd like to thank everyone involved in the publishing process for their efforts in making this book a reality. Their efforts, from copyediting to advertising, made the project what it is today.

Finally, I'd like to express my gratitude to everyone who has shown me unconditional love and encouragement throughout my life. Their support was crucial to the completion of this book. I appreciate your help with this endeavour and your continued interest in my career.

CHAPTER 1: INTRODUCTION TO NETWORKING AND C++

Chapter Overview

In this chapter, you'll start your exploration into the world of C++ for networking by learning why C++ is still a top choice for building fast, reliable, and scalable network applications. You'll see how the language's main strengths, performance, control, and deep system access, give you unique power over every detail of network communication, from packets and sockets to full-featured servers.

As you read through the chapter, it'll show you how the evolution from early C++ to the current C++23 standard has made network code safer and more reliable, and also easier to write and maintain. We'll be exploring each major advancement in the language, from memory safety to concurrent programming, in context to show you exactly how these features translate into practical networking tasks. You'll look at the fundamentals of C++ from the point of view of a network programmer, building your skills in handling types, variables, memory, and data structures in ways that really matter for networking projects in the real world.

The chapter will also show you the essential networking libraries that you'll use a lot in the book, so you can get a sneak peek at the powerful tools that can make your coding journey easier. Finally, you'll set up your whole C++ development environment on Windows, creating a clear and reusable project structure so you're ready to build, test, and expand your own networking projects with confidence as you move through each chapter of the book.

Understanding C++ for Networking

If you join a networking or engineering team, you'll probably notice something interesting: even with all the excitement about new languages, C++ is still the go-to. If we're building a packet sniffer, a high-frequency router, or even a modern VPN, C++ gives us direct access to the metal, raw sockets, buffers, real-time system calls. When it comes to milliseconds and bytes, C++ isn't just tradition, it's the go-to choice. It's the foundation.

C++ Evolving with Networking

When I first came across C++ code from the '90s or early 2000s, I saw a lot of manual memory management, pointers, and maybe even the occasional buffer overflow waiting to happen. That's how the networking bigwigs did it back in the day. But if you and I look at what happened with C++11, everything starts to change. All of a sudden, smart pointers let us hand off memory safely between a server's packet processor and its main event loop. You won't have to stress about double frees or leaks when you've got a thousand socket connections going at once. Move semantics are here, and now you're dealing with buffers and packet structs at wire speed, no copies to hold you up. For the first time, you can start a thread or two with just a couple of lines, letting your server scale without any external threading library.

A few years later, C++14 and C++17 quietly sneak in new tricks. You will write an async handler using lambdas so you don't need to define a whole new class just to process a TCP packet. You might use **std::optional** to handle situations where a DNS response is missing a field, or **std::string_view** when you need to parse a buffer without copying a single byte, absolutely essential when your application is sitting on a 10Gbps interface and memory allocations become your real bottleneck.

When we hit C++20, everything gets even more exciting for you as a network engineer. Coroutines allow us to handle thousands of live connections, all with code that reads like step-by-step logic, not a maze of callbacks. Imagine being able to **co_await** a read from the socket, your logic waits, but your thread doesn't. At the same time, **std::span** means you're finally able to manipulate byte buffers in a type-safe, zero-copy way, which helps both performance and correctness. And with C++23, we get features that make network code safer, clearer, and more maintainable than ever. Pattern matching, extended constexpr, and even more powerful ranges, suddenly your packet parsers and protocol state machines aren't just faster; they're easier to reason about and extend. You can enforce invariants at compile time, preventing whole classes of errors before you even hit build.

Modern C++ Building Networks

Let's get practical. If you walk into a company building load balancers, SDN switches, or distributed file systems, you will see C++ everywhere. From the fast path in a telecom core router to open-source powerhouses like Wireshark or Zeek, it's C++ that keeps the packets moving. AWS, Google, and Azure run vast amounts of C++ code for load balancing, edge nodes, and high-throughput backend services. Even the Linux kernel's user space networking tools, which you might be using daily, often rely on C++ for anything that isn't strictly in C. Financial trading, telecom, cloud, IoT, automotive, everywhere that packets move fast and reliability matters, teams reach for C++. Not just because "that's what we've always done," but because every new C++ standard brings in new tools, patterns, and safety nets for the job.

So, what does all this evolution mean for you, hands-on? Let's say you're tasked with building an HTTP/3 server. In classic C++, you'd be wrestling with pointers and custom buffer classes. Today, you'd reach for **std::vector<std::byte>**, smart pointers, and maybe a coroutine-based networking stack. Your main server loop is not a spaghetti of nested callbacks but a clean sequence of awaits, much easier to follow, debug, and extend. If you wish to handle optional headers or support multiple protocol versions, then there is **std::optional**, **std::variant**, and structured bindings to keep your logic readable and tight. Likewise, if we want to add metrics or handle errors gracefully? Then the new error handling and formatting facilities make it straightforward to log and diagnose every edge case without missing a beat.

Each time you learn a new C++ feature, you add another tool in your belt. The modern standards let you write expressive, efficient, and safe networked applications without giving up the performance or low-level access you need for the toughest jobs. The more you adopt these features, the more you'll find your code is not just faster, but also clearer, more robust, and easier to share with your team.

Refreshing C++ Basics

Now, let us revisit the basics before we dive into detail. When you prepare to tackle network programming in C++, it's tempting to jump right into sockets and protocols. But trust me, having a rock-solid grasp of the basics will save you hours of debugging and give you the kind of confidence that shows up in every line of your code.

Variables and Types

At the core, you will find that C++ is all about types, variables, and structure. Every time you declare an **int**, a **double**, or a **std::string**, you're defining exactly how your program interacts with memory. This level of control isn't just academic, it matters when you're parsing binary packets, aligning data for a protocol, or managing buffers for high-speed I/O.

You will remember that every C++ program starts with a **main()** function. This is the entry point where execution begins. As you write networking utilities, you will quickly appreciate how a clear, minimal **main()** makes it easy to test and iterate. Even a tiny UDP echo server or a packet parser starts with just this:

```
#include <iostream>

int main() {

    std::cout << "Networking begins here!" << std::endl;

    return 0;

}
```

The best thing to use for networking is to have a list of your types. When you're reading from a socket, each byte you receive needs to be interpreted as the right kind of data, like an integer, a floating point number, or just a chunk of bytes. The C++ gives you precise types, from simple **int** and **char** up to the full power of **std::vector<uint8_t>** for raw packet data.

When you declare a variable like **uint16_t port = 8080;**, you're telling your compiler to use exactly 16 bits. That's not just neat, it's essential when building portable protocol handlers that work across different architectures. You never want to assume **int** means the same thing everywhere. The standard types in **<cstdint>** like **uint8_t**, **uint16_t**, and **uint32_t** will help keep your code portable and bug-free.

Pointers, References and Memory

The cool thing about C++ is that it lets you manage memory directly. It might seem a bit intimidating at first, but that's actually one of the main reasons C++ is great for networking. When you get a packet, you usually work with a pointer to a buffer. You can use pointers to parse, inspect, and modify data in place, and do it all at top speed.

However, the raw pointers can lead to trouble. As you adopt modern C++, you will see that smart pointers, like **std::unique_ptr** and **std::shared_ptr**, let you manage resources safely. In a network server, you might use a smart pointer to own a socket object or a buffer, knowing it will get cleaned up automatically when you're done.

```
#include <memory>

#include <vector>

std::unique_ptr<std::vector<uint8_t>> buffer =
std::make_unique<std::vector<uint8_t>>(1024);
```

This style isn't just cleaner. It means fewer memory leaks, safer error handling, and more robust networking code.

Arrays, Strings, and Buffer Management

We're used to working with arrays in C++, but in networking, you quickly run into buffers. Those are blocks of raw bytes you read from the wire. You might receive a packet as an array like **uint8_t buffer[1500];** or, more commonly in modern C++, as a **std::vector<uint8_t>** which makes it easy to resize, slice, and process your incoming and outgoing data.

For text, C++ offers both classic C-style strings (**char[]**) and the safer, more flexible **std::string** class. If you're parsing HTTP headers or building custom messages, you will find **std::string_view** extremely useful. It lets you reference slices of data without copying, essential for performance in tight loops or real-time packet inspection.

Control Flow, Logic and Decisions

Every network application needs to react to the data it receives. Control structures like **if**, **switch**, **for**, and **while** let you write logic that inspects packets, branches based on protocol headers, and loops through streams of data. When you write a server that checks if a packet type is valid or loops until all bytes are received, you're using the same control flow you learned at the start, but now, with purpose.

```
for (size_t i = 0; i < packet.size(); ++i) {
    if (packet[i] == target_byte) {
        // Handle protocol marker
    }
}
```

Functions and Modularity

The networking projects I've worked on have grown really fast. It's like you can break your program down into logical pieces. You can have one function to parse a header, another to handle a connection, and another to log errors. This modularity is key to keeping your networking code organized and testable, especially as projects grow.

Modern C++ lets you take this even further with lambda functions. These let you pass around small blocks of logic, which is great for asynchronous handlers, callbacks, or event-driven code.

```
auto handler = [](const std::vector<uint8_t>& data) {
    // process packet
};
```

When you need to maintain tables of open connections, lists of pending packets, or sets of protocol handlers, the Standard Template Library (STL) steps in. **`std::vector`**, **`std::map`**, **`std::unordered_map`**, and **`std::set`** are used constantly in networking. You might use a **`std::map<IPAddress, Connection>`** to track active sessions, or a **`std::vector<uint8_t>`** for a rolling buffer. These containers save you from reinventing the wheel, letting you focus on your actual networking logic.

C++ Libraries for Networking

As you dive into network programming, you will quickly see that the C++ standard library doesn't include networking out of the box. That's where powerful third-party libraries come in, giving you modern, efficient tools to handle sockets, protocols, and async operations.

Boost.Asio

The Boost.Asio is where many C++ networking adventures begin. With Asio, you can open sockets, accept connections, read and write data, and handle everything asynchronously. You will appreciate its cross-platform reliability, whether you're on Linux, Windows, or macOS, your code runs with almost no changes.

Suppose you're building a TCP echo server. With Boost.Asio, you set up an **`io_context`**, create an acceptor, and let the library handle connections as they come in. You can process requests as callbacks, use coroutines, or integrate with threads, whatever fits your application best. With C++20 and later, the Asio's coroutine support lets you write code that looks synchronous but is fully asynchronous under the hood. This means you can process each network event step-by-step, without deeply nested callbacks.

POCO C++ Libraries

When you're ready to move beyond raw sockets, POCO gives you higher-level abstractions for everything from HTTP and FTP to SMTP and WebSocket servers. You can spin up a web server, process REST APIs, or connect to IoT devices without reimplementing the protocol details yourself. You might use POCO's **`Net`** library to create a secure HTTPS server or its data components to talk to SQL databases right from your networking code. The cross-platform focus of POCO makes it ideal when your project must run reliably everywhere.

cURLpp

If your networking project needs to interact with web APIs or perform file transfers, cURLpp is your go-to. As a modern C++ wrapper around the venerable cURL library, it lets you issue HTTP requests, download or upload files, and manage complex protocol options, all with clean, readable C++ code. The cURLpp shines when you need to handle cookies, manage authentication, or interact with web services as part of your networking logic. You get all the power of cURL, support for dozens of protocols, SSL/TLS, robust error handling, presented in an interface that feels natural for C++.

And as you build your networking skills, you'll see that using strong libraries saves time, reduces errors, and lets you focus on solving real problems. If you're writing a quick utility, building a big server, or trying out new protocols, Boost.Asio, POCO, and cURLpp will make your project so much easier and more fun.

Setting up C++ Environment

Compiler and Development Environment

To get started with modern C++, I'd recommend a toolchain that gives you all the features of C++23 and a development environment that feels intuitive. You can install MinGW-w64 for GCC and VS Code as your IDE.

Install MinGW-w64

This is quite easy as you just have to install the latest MinGW-w64 installer and run it. You then choose the architecture (x86_64), threads (posix), and exception (seh), then let it install to a folder like **`C:\mingw-w64`**.

Once complete, add **`C:\mingw-w64\bin`** to your system PATH, so you can access **`g++`** from anywhere in the command prompt.

Install VS Code

This is another very easy to get it installed, as you simply have to visit the VS Code website, download the Windows installer, and install. Then, after you launch VS Code, you need to go to Extensions, then search for "C/C++" and install it. This gives you powerful syntax highlighting, code navigation, error checking, and even graphical debugging.

Sample Project Structure

After the installation, we can easily lay out our first real C++ networking project. For this, at first, open the home directory, and inside **Projects**, create a folder called **cpp-networking-demo**.

Inside this (cpp-networking-demo) folder, we then set up a structure like:

- **src/** - Contains all C++ source files (.cpp)
- **include/** - Houses custom header files (.h/.hpp)
- **libs/** - External dependencies and third-party libraries
- **build/** - Build artifacts, object files, and executables
- **CMakeLists.txt** - CMake configuration for cross-platform builds
- **README.md** - Project documentation and setup instructions

This setup you will put all your C++ source code into **src**, headers into **include**, and link to third-party libraries from **libs**. The **build** folder keeps your compiled binaries separate, so you don't clutter your codebase. If you decide to use CMake (highly recommended for larger projects), **CMakeLists.txt** at the root lets you configure builds for Windows and other platforms seamlessly.

Following is how a basic **main.cpp** might look in your project:

```
#include <iostream>
#include "network_utils.h"
int main() {
    std::cout << "Your C++ Networking Project Environment is
Ready!" << std::endl;
    // Future networking code goes here
    return 0;
}
```

And the below is the **network_utils.h** header:

```
#pragma once
void show_network_message();
```

Installing and Configuring Libraries

Whenever you need Boost.Asio, POCO, or cURLpp, download them into your **libs** directory. Extract and build each library according to its Windows instructions, and then configure your build system (either CMake or direct compiler flags) to include headers from

libs/boost_1_xx_x, **libs/poco**, or **libs/curlpp**. You won't have to repeat this installation for every new project, just reference your existing **libs** folder. This way, you avoid setup headaches and can jump straight into coding.

If you choose to use CMake (strongly suggested as projects grow), a minimal **CMakeLists.txt** might look like this:

```
cmake_minimum_required(VERSION 3.15)
project(cpp_networking_demo)
set(CMAKE_CXX_STANDARD 23)
include_directories(include)
add_executable(cpp_networking_demo src/main.cpp)
```

You will extend this file later as you add libraries and more source files.

After all this, we must do a quick test of thr setup, for which, we will open a terminal inside our project directory and run the following:

```
g++ -std=c++23 -Iinclude src/main.cpp -o build/demo.exe
.\build\demo.exe
```

If everything prints as expected, your environment and structure are working. Every new example in this book will assume you've set up your projects just like this, so you can focus on learning and experimenting, not on tracking down misplaced files or mysterious build errors.

With this setup, you're not just following a checklist, you're building a solid foundation for everything you will do as a network programmer in C++. Each new feature, each demo, and every library integrates smoothly. You will find it's easier to collaborate, test, and grow your codebase, no matter how complex your networking tools become.

Summary

Throughout this chapter, you explored the role of C++ in networking, understanding why it remains a foundational language for building networked systems, tools, and applications. The evolution of C++ standards, from its origins to C++23, was woven into practical examples, showing how features such as smart pointers, move semantics, coroutines, and new data types have made modern networking code safer, faster, and easier to maintain. The learnings included a refresher on core C++ concepts, focusing on types, variables, memory management, arrays, and modular programming, always tying these basics back to real networking scenarios. You also learned how precise type choices, effective use of pointers, and standard library containers directly support packet processing and protocol implementation.

The learnings introduced key libraries, Boost.Asio, POCO, and cURLpp, demonstrating how these tools empower professionals to build robust, scalable networked software. The chapter also provided a guided setup for a modern C++ development environment on Windows, complete with a practical, professional project structure. By following this approach, you gained the skills and confidence to write, organize, and test C++ networking projects effectively, building a solid foundation for all upcoming practical and theoretical content in the book.

Chapter 2: Understanding TCP and UDP

Chapter Overview

In this chapter, you'll dive into the essential protocols that form the backbone of network communication. You'll start by learning how protocol stacks work, from the link layer all the way up to the application layer, and discover why each layer plays a unique role in delivering data across local and global networks. You'll get to grips with both Transmission Control Protocol (TCP) and User Datagram Protocol (UDP), learning not just how they work, but also when and why to use each one. You'll learn about the inner workings of TCP, how it establishes connections, ensures reliable delivery, and controls flow. You'll also see how all of this works together to help you build strong, session-oriented applications.

Next, is that you dive deeper into UDP's stateless, fast messaging model, and learn about the trade-offs between speed and reliability that shape modern, real-time software. You'll get to grips with the basics of socket programming and see how sockets provide a direct interface between your C++ code and the network. You'll gradually write both TCP and UDP clients and servers, mastering the core functions, error handling, and best practices that ensure your applications perform well in real-world conditions. When you're done with this chapter, you'll have the know-how to put together, run, and fix networked programs like a pro. This gets you ready to dive into the more advanced stuff and real-world projects as you make your way through the book.

Internet Protocols Basics

Every networked application you build relies on well-defined protocols to send and receive data across unreliable, complex networks. The protocols aren't just a formality, they determine how your packets are structured, how endpoints identify and handle errors, and how different devices agree on everything from addressing to retransmission.

Protocol Layers

You can think of protocol layers as a stack. Each layer handles a different part such as:

- The **Physical/Link Layer** delivers raw bits between physical devices (Ethernet, Wi-Fi).
- The **Network Layer** handles addressing and routing (IP, ICMP).
- The **Transport Layer** provides end-to-end communication between hosts (TCP, UDP).
- And, the last **application Layer** implements specific network services (HTTP, FTP, DNS, SMTP).

Our job as a C++ developer is mostly at the transport and application layers, crafting programs that send, receive, and process data using TCP, UDP, and higher-level protocols.

Why Protocols?

When you write code that sends a request to a web server, your message passes through several protocol layers. For example, you might use HTTP to request a page. HTTP forms the message, but TCP ensures reliable delivery, while IP finds a route to the server, and Ethernet (or Wi-Fi) gets it onto the wire.

And, the interoperability is vital as, when your C++ program sends a TCP packet, it must conform precisely to what the server expects, or the server won't recognize it. Protocols define every byte, from header fields to error correction, so a packet generated on Linux will be correctly interpreted on Windows, macOS, or even an embedded IoT board.

In most real-world C++ networking, we use and depend upon:

- **TCP** for reliable, connection-oriented communication. Powers HTTP, HTTPS, FTP, SSH.
- **UDP** for fast, connectionless delivery. Critical for DNS, VoIP, video streaming, and real-time games.
- **ICMP** when we want to handle diagnostic tasks like ping.
- And, **Application Protocols** including HTTP, SMTP, POP3, MQTT, etc., each with their own format layered over TCP/UDP.

Most of the time, you'll be using high-level libraries, inspecting raw packet headers, handling byte ordering, and debugging network traces with Wireshark. And if you get the hang of the underlying protocols, you can build solid C++ applications that work like a charm, no matter where you are.

Transmission Control Protocol (TCP) Deep Dive

When you code with TCP in C++, you're working with a protocol engineered for reliability, sequencing, and flow control, all built atop a fundamentally unreliable network.

TCP Segment Structure

A TCP segment is the basic unit exchanged between sender and receiver. The segment contains a header (minimum 20 bytes) and optional data. Here's what you will see in every TCP header:

Field	Size (bits)	Purpose
Source Port	16	Sender's port number
Destination Port	16	Receiver's port number

Sequence Number	32	Byte index of the first byte in this segment
Acknowledgment Number	32	Next expected byte from peer
Data Offset	4	Header length (in 32-bit words)
Flags	6	URG, ACK, PSH, RST, SYN, FIN
Window Size	16	How much data the sender is willing to receive
Checksum	16	Error checking for header and data
Urgent Pointer	16	Only if URG is set (rare in practice)
Options/Padding	Variable	MSS, Window Scaling, Timestamps, etc.

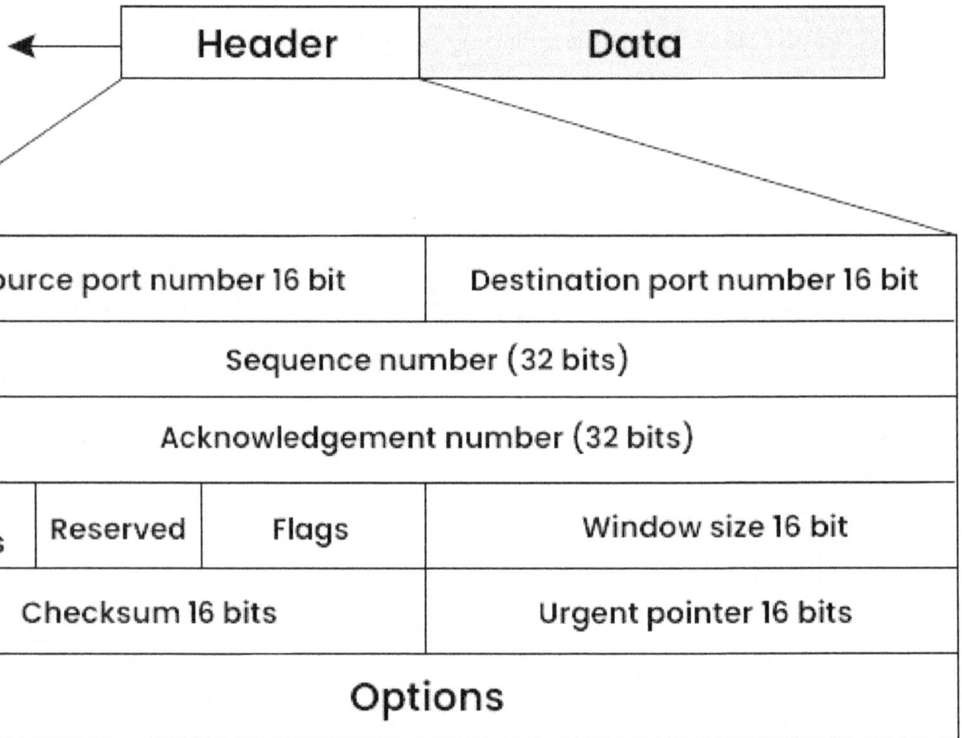

Fig 2.1 TCP Header

(Source: https://www.pynetlabs.com/transmission-control-protocol-tcp-header/)

The most important thing is that every time we use C++ to read or send data over TCP, our networking stack is assembling and parsing these headers for us.

Three-Way Handshake

The TCP needs a handshake to open a connection, wherein:

- The client sends a TCP segment with the **SYN** flag set to start the connection and suggest an initial sequence number.
- The server replies with its own **SYN-ACK** and acknowledges the client's sequence.
- Then the client sends an **ACK**, and both sides are ready to transmit data.

You can actually observe these flags using Wireshark or by inspecting socket states in C++.

You also must know that the TCP breaks large messages into segments. Each byte is numbered using the sequence field. As segments arrive, the receiver checks sequence numbers and reorders out-of-sequence segments, discarding duplicates and asking for retransmission of missing data. For example, if your server sends "Hello, world!" in two segments, TCP will ensure the client receives them in order, even if the packets arrive out of sequence. Apart from this, for every segment received, the peer sends back an acknowledgment (ACK) with the next expected byte. If no ACK arrives within a timeout, the TCP then resends the missing data. And because of this, you will rarely experience the data loss in TCP-based C++ applications.

So, when you create a TCP server or client in C++, you work with sockets that encapsulate all this logic. The libraries like Boost.Asio let you control timeouts, buffer sizes, and manage errors, while the OS handles all protocol-level details. But, understanding how sequence numbers, ACKs, and retransmissions work gives you a huge advantage when diagnosing network issues or building robust custom protocols.

User Datagram Protocol (UDP) Deep Dive

When we are stepping into UDP, we are actually choosing the simplest possible model for network communication. Unlike TCP, there's no setup, no session, no guarantee, just a direct shot from sender to receiver. So, in C++ code, you can fire off a datagram with a single call, and it'll be on its way instantly, even if the other side isn't listening.

UDP Packet Structure

We will try to look at a UDP datagram more closely. The header is only **8 bytes**, much lighter than TCP. Here's how it's laid out:

Field	Size (bits)	Purpose
Source Port	16	Identifies sender application
Destination Port	16	Identifies target application

Length	16	Total size (header + payload, in bytes)
Checksum	16	Error-checks header and data (mandatory for IPv6)

After the header, you get your data, whatever payload your application sends. There are no sequence numbers, no acknowledgments, and no fields for window size or flags. This leanness means less time assembling and parsing, and almost no processing needed by routers and endpoints. Your packet is free to go, fast.

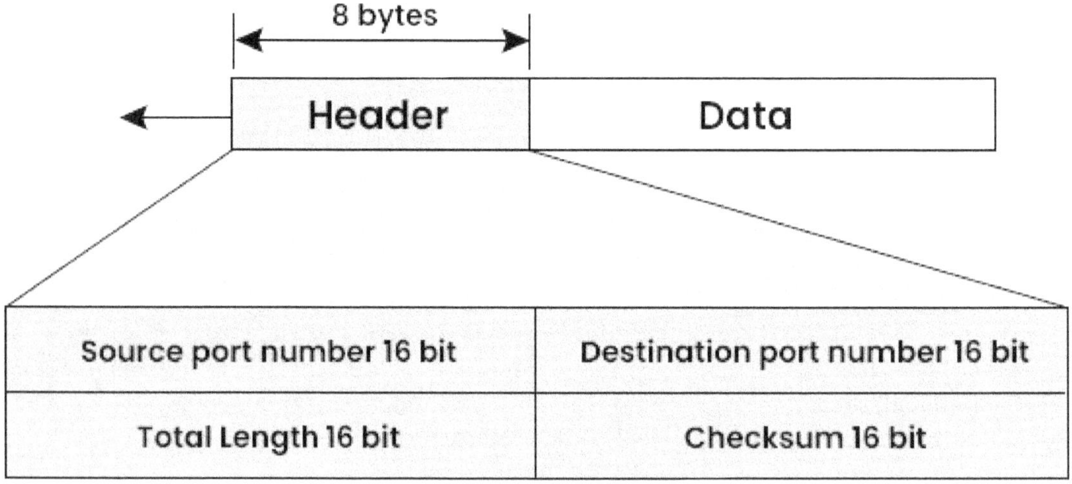

Fig 2.2 UDP Header

(https://www.pynetlabs.com/transport-layer-protocols/)

Connectionless, Stateless Operation

With UDP, every datagram stands alone. There's no handshake before sending data. If you want to send ten packets to ten different hosts, you can do so with ten independent calls, no connection setup, no teardown, no per-client state on the server.

This is ideal for:

1. Broadcasts (one-to-all) and multicasts (one-to-many) on LANs.
2. High-volume, real-time telemetry where the latest data matters more than missing a few packets.
3. Protocols where the application handles its own logic for missing, duplicated, or out-of-order data.

Since the UDP is stateless, the server isn't burdened by thousands of open connections, it just listens and responds as needed.

Fragmentation and Error Handling

The UDP datagrams are limited by the underlying network's maximum transmission unit (MTU), often 1500 bytes on Ethernet. If your message is larger, it can be fragmented at the IP layer. However, fragmentation increases risk: if even one fragment is lost, the entire datagram is discarded. For reliability, keep datagrams within typical MTU limits, and avoid fragmentation where possible.

In addition, the checksum field checks for corruption in transit. So, if a packet arrives with a bad checksum, it's simply discarded, no request for retransmission, no notification to sender or receiver. If you want to know whether data made it, you must build acknowledgments into your application logic.

In C++, working with UDP means, creating a socket of type **SOCK_DGRAM**, binding the socket to a port (on the server), using the **`sendto()`** or **`async_send_to()`** to transmit data to any address/port, and then receiving packets with **`recvfrom()`** or **`async_receive_from()`**.

There is no connect(), listen(), or accept(), it is just simply pure immediate messaging. This simplicity makes UDP attractive for real-time scenarios such as **Voice and video calls, Online gaming, DNS, and Sensor data and telemetry.**

When to use TCP or UDP?

The TCP and UDP embody two completely different networking philosophies. The TCP believes in reliability, order, and correctness. It tracks every byte, ensures nothing gets lost, and adjusts transmission rates to match network and endpoint capacity. And, the UDP believes in speed, simplicity, and "fire and forget" delivery. It does not track sessions, never resends, and lets the application decide what to do if something is missing.

Protocol Mechanics Difference

Feature	TCP	UDP
Connection	Required (handshake: SYN, SYN-ACK, ACK)	None (just send packets)
Delivery Guarantee	Yes (ACKs, retransmits, sequence/order)	No guarantee, no retransmits
Data Format	Stream (continuous bytes)	Datagram (individual messages)

Overhead	Higher (20–60+ byte header, session state, control)	Minimal (8-byte header, stateless)
Flow/Congestion Ctrl	Built-in	None
Error Recovery	Yes (retransmits, reordering)	No (application handles it)
Use Cases	Web, file transfer, email, SSH, DB	Streaming, games, DNS, VoIP, sensors

Technical Decision Workflow

If you choose **TCP**, your C++ code will manage a connection-oriented socket (**`SOCK_STREAM`**). This means each **`connect()`** call results in a persistent virtual circuit: your OS tracks the session state, buffers, and retransmits as needed. Every byte you send is split into segments, each tagged with a sequence number and acknowledged by the receiver. TCP flow and congestion control algorithms ensure your sender doesn't overwhelm the receiver or the network. You can control socket timeouts, buffer sizes, and even tweak Nagle's algorithm (TCP_NODELAY) if you need to send small packets instantly.

When you work with **UDP**, you use a datagram socket (**`SOCK_DGRAM`**). There is no handshake or connection phase. Every call to **`sendto()`** transmits a self-contained message, with source/destination port and IP, plus a 16-bit UDP checksum for error detection. There are no sequence numbers, no retransmissions, no guarantees. Your code may need to track packet ordering, loss, or implement retries and application-level acknowledgments. UDP is ideal if your packets are small (ideally less than the typical MTU, e.g., 1472 bytes for Ethernet), and you want to broadcast or multicast data with minimal resource use.

Proven TCP and UDP Use-cases

Suppose your program needs to transfer a big file, update a database, or run a login session. You can't risk losing a single packet or mixing up the order. TCP is your safety-first protocol. The moment you call **`connect()`** in your C++ code, your machine and the server go through a three-way handshake, SYN, SYN-ACK, ACK, before any real data moves. From then on, every segment carries a sequence number, and every received byte is acknowledged. If anything goes missing, TCP quietly fills in the gaps. You don't have to track packet order or worry about duplicates. That's why you will see TCP underneath your web browsers, emails, and version control tools, it's built to guarantee delivery.

But let's flip the script. Maybe your app is a real-time sensor, a video streamer, or a multiplayer game. If a few data points get lost, the show must go on! Here's where UDP shines. There's no handshake, no session to manage, each call to **`sendto()`** in your C++ code fires off a standalone message. The OS doesn't care if the other side is listening. The network doesn't wait for acknowledgments. You get maximum speed, minimal delay, and complete freedom to broadcast, multicast, or send one-off bursts. Your responsibility: if you need reliability or order, you build that logic in your application layer. If it's okay to drop an update now and then, UDP's simplicity will serve you well.

You will see this decision in every project. Banking and file transfer? Always TCP. Live audio or movement updates? Nearly always UDP. Sometimes, you will even mix both, chat messages over TCP, but game events or telemetry over UDP. So here, you as a C++ developer has to make that call with your user's needs in mind, and understand how it shapes every send, receive, and error-handling path you build.

Sockets and Socket Programming

The sockets are the hands-on part of networking, where your C++ code meets the internet head-on. It can be thought of as a virtual endpoint that allows your program to connect to another program across a network. It is very much like opening a communication channel where both ends can exchange data in a structured way. As soon as you create a socket, you've opened a two-way door to the world, ready to send or receive packets. So, for our system, we will primarily work with Winsock library, which offers a set of functions tailored for socket programming. Winsock is essentially Microsoft's implementation of the socket interface but aligns closely with the standards that originated in the Berkeley sockets API on Unix systems.

Programming Sockets

We will walk through a real example together. Suppose you want to build a TCP server. You call **`socket(AF_INET, SOCK_STREAM, 0)`**, and the OS hands you a socket descriptor, a number representing your end of the connection.

```
// TCP socket (IPv4)
int sockfd = socket(AF_INET, SOCK_STREAM, 0);
// UDP socket (IPv4)
int udpfd = socket(AF_INET, SOCK_DGRAM, 0);
```

For a server, you will bind the socket to a local IP and port:

```
struct sockaddr_in addr;
addr.sin_family = AF_INET;
addr.sin_addr.s_addr = INADDR_ANY;
addr.sin_port = htons(12345);
bind(sockfd, (struct sockaddr*)&addr, sizeof(addr));
```

For TCP, you listen for connections and accept them:

```
listen(sockfd, SOMAXCONN);
int clientfd = accept(sockfd, NULL, NULL);
```

And for UDP, you simply call **recvfrom()** to receive packets from any sender, and use **sendto()** to reply:

```
char buffer[1500];
struct sockaddr_in sender_addr;
socklen_t addrlen = sizeof(sender_addr);
ssize_t n = recvfrom(udpfd, buffer, sizeof(buffer), 0,
                     (struct sockaddr*)&sender_addr,
&addrlen);
```

In the above, the TCP provides stream-oriented functions (**send()**, **recv()**), where you must be prepared for partial sends/receives and handle the case where data is split across multiple reads. UDP, on the other hand, guarantees each call to **recvfrom()** returns a single datagram; if the buffer is too small, the rest is discarded.

Also, the sockets can be customized using **setsockopt()**, for example, adjusting send/receive buffer size, enabling keepalive, or setting non-blocking mode. While using C++, you must check return codes for every call; since the network errors are frequent and must be handled explicitly.

If you use Boost.Asio, you need to wrap the sockets in **ip::tcp::socket** or **ip::udp::socket** classes. The asynchronous methods (**async_read_some**, **async_send_to**) allow your server to process many connections or datagrams in parallel, using a single thread or a thread pool, with handlers for completion and errors. Every C++ network application you build, debug, or optimize will use these tools, so getting comfortable at this level pays off in every project.

Useful Socket Programming Techniques

Most of the successful networked applications are built on careful, defensive socket programming. I will teach you precisely some of the best practices so you can also build such strong sockets into your workflow.

Rigorous Error Checking

In your original TCP server code, each step, from **WSAStartup** to **socket()**, **bind()**, **listen()**, **accept()**, **recv()**, and **send()**, should be checked for failure. For example, after creating the listening socket:

```
SOCKET listenSock = socket(AF_INET, SOCK_STREAM, 0);
```

```
if (listenSock == INVALID_SOCKET) {
    std::cerr << "Socket creation failed: " <<
WSAGetLastError() << std::endl;
    WSACleanup();
    return 1;
}
```

Apply similar checks after every critical call. On errors, log the problem, clean up, and avoid undefined behavior.

Prompt Resource Cleanup

Whenever your server or client finishes using a socket, whether due to success, error, or an exception, close it promptly. In more advanced programs, wrap sockets in a class that calls **`closesocket()`** automatically when destroyed, ensuring you never leave dangling sockets:

```
struct ScopedSocket {
    SOCKET sock;
    ScopedSocket(SOCKET s) : sock(s) {}
    ~ScopedSocket() { if (sock != INVALID_SOCKET)
closesocket(sock); }
};
```

Use this for both the listening and client sockets.

Timeouts and Blocking Control

By default, operations like **`recv()`** or **`accept()`** will block forever if no data arrives. For real servers, set reasonable timeouts to avoid hanging on dead connections:

```
int timeout = 5000; // milliseconds
setsockopt(clientSock, SOL_SOCKET, SO_RCVTIMEO,
(char*)&timeout, sizeof(timeout));
```

This way, your program can detect stale clients and handle them gracefully.

Non-blocking and Asynchronous Handling

If you anticipate handling multiple clients or want your server to stay responsive, enable non-blocking mode:

```
u_long mode = 1;
ioctlsocket(listenSock, FIONBIO, &mode);
```

Alternatively, switch to event-driven libraries like Boost.Asio to handle many sockets in a single thread, using callbacks for I/O readiness.

Partial Sends and Receives

TCP's **send()** and **recv()** may transfer less than the requested number of bytes, especially on busy networks. Always use loops to ensure all data is processed. In your server:

```
int totalSent = 0;
while (totalSent < bytesReceived) {
    int sent = send(clientSock, buffer + totalSent,
bytesReceived - totalSent, 0);
    if (sent <= 0) { /* handle error */ break; }
    totalSent += sent;
}
```

For clients, use a similar loop when sending large buffers.

Buffer Validation and Input Sanitization

Never trust network input. If you expect at most 1024 bytes, but **recv()** returns more or a malformed request, always validate and cap lengths before processing or responding:

```
if (bytesReceived > 0 && bytesReceived <= sizeof(buffer)) {
    // Safe to process
} else {
    // Malformed or malicious data; drop or log
}
```

When debugging, enable verbose logs to track down elusive bugs or performance issues. These practices future-proof your code for real production deployments, handling edge cases, scaling to many clients, recovering from faults, and defending against malformed traffic.

TCP Client-Server Socket Programming

The whole point of network programming is to get two programs to talk to each other over the network, and TCP makes that happen by setting up a connection, making sure everything gets delivered in the right order, and giving you a simple interface that's based on streams. We'll build both the server and the client, and we'll make sure to explain every step.

Building a TCP Server

We will start with writing a simple TCP echo server, something that accepts connections, receives messages, and sends them right back. In C++, the workflow is quite methodical and reasonable:

1. **Create a socket** with **`AF_INET`**, **`SOCK_STREAM`**, and protocol 0.
2. **Bind** it to a local IP and port, making your server visible.
3. **Listen** for incoming connections.
4. **Accept** a client connection, which gives you a dedicated socket for that session.
5. **Read and write** as needed.
6. **Close** both client and server sockets when done.

Now, let us see the above step-wise workflow in the following script:

```
#include <winsock2.h>
#include <iostream>
#pragma comment(lib, "ws2_32.lib")
int main() {
    WSADATA wsa;
    WSAStartup(MAKEWORD(2,2), &wsa);
    SOCKET listenSock = socket(AF_INET, SOCK_STREAM, 0);
    sockaddr_in serverAddr = {};
    serverAddr.sin_family = AF_INET;
    serverAddr.sin_addr.s_addr = INADDR_ANY;
    serverAddr.sin_port = htons(8080);
    bind(listenSock, (sockaddr*)&serverAddr,
sizeof(serverAddr));
    listen(listenSock, SOMAXCONN);
    std::cout << "Waiting for a connection..." << std::endl;
    SOCKET clientSock = accept(listenSock, nullptr, nullptr);
    char buffer[1024];
    int bytesReceived = recv(clientSock, buffer,
sizeof(buffer), 0);
    if (bytesReceived > 0) {
```

```
        send(clientSock, buffer, bytesReceived, 0);
    }
    closesocket(clientSock);
    closesocket(listenSock);
    WSACleanup();
    return 0;
}
```

In the above, each function here plays a crucial role. **accept()** blocks until a client connects. Afterward, **recv()** waits for data, and **send()** writes it back. TCP handles all reliability, packet fragmentation, and ordering behind the scenes.

Writing a TCP Client

On the client side, we will connect to the server, send a message, and wait for the echo.

```
#include <winsock2.h>
#include <iostream>
#pragma comment(lib, "ws2_32.lib")
int main() {
    WSADATA wsa;
    WSAStartup(MAKEWORD(2,2), &wsa);
    SOCKET sock = socket(AF_INET, SOCK_STREAM, 0);
    sockaddr_in serverAddr = {};
    serverAddr.sin_family = AF_INET;
    serverAddr.sin_addr.s_addr = inet_addr("127.0.0.1");
    serverAddr.sin_port = htons(8080);
    connect(sock, (sockaddr*)&serverAddr, sizeof(serverAddr));
    const char* message = "Hello TCP Server!";
    send(sock, message, strlen(message), 0);
    char buffer[1024];
    int bytesReceived = recv(sock, buffer, sizeof(buffer), 0);
    if (bytesReceived > 0) {
```

```
        std::cout << "Echo from server: ";
        std::cout.write(buffer, bytesReceived);
        std::cout << std::endl;
    }
    closesocket(sock);
    WSACleanup();
    return 0;
}
```

After the handshake, the connection persists for as many exchanges as you need. Each read and write is a reliable, ordered stream, ideal for all cases where correctness matters.

UDP Client-Server Socket Programming

The UDP offers an entirely different model. There's no handshake, no ongoing connection, just fire-and-forget messages. It's a perfect fit for scenarios where speed is vital, and occasional loss is acceptable.

Creating a UDP Server

We will create a UDP server that simply listens on a port and responds to each incoming datagram, always including the sender's address for replies. Following is the script:

```
#include <winsock2.h>
#include <iostream>
#pragma comment(lib, "ws2_32.lib")
int main() {
    WSADATA wsa;
    WSAStartup(MAKEWORD(2,2), &wsa);
    SOCKET sock = socket(AF_INET, SOCK_DGRAM, 0);
    sockaddr_in serverAddr = {};
    serverAddr.sin_family = AF_INET;
    serverAddr.sin_addr.s_addr = INADDR_ANY;
    serverAddr.sin_port = htons(9090);
    bind(sock, (sockaddr*)&serverAddr, sizeof(serverAddr));
```

```
    char buffer[1024];
    sockaddr_in clientAddr;
    int clientLen = sizeof(clientAddr);
    int bytesReceived = recvfrom(sock, buffer, sizeof(buffer),
0,
                                (sockaddr*)&clientAddr,
&clientLen);
    if (bytesReceived > 0) {
        sendto(sock, buffer, bytesReceived, 0,
               (sockaddr*)&clientAddr, clientLen);
    }
    closesocket(sock);
    WSACleanup();
    return 0;
}
```

Now if you notice in the above, there's no accept, no listen. Any client can send, at any time, from anywhere. Every packet is an isolated event.

Creating a UDP Client

The client sends a message to the server, waits for the response, and is done. It never "connects" in the TCP sense.

```
#include <winsock2.h>
#include <iostream>
#pragma comment(lib, "ws2_32.lib")
int main() {
    WSADATA wsa;
    WSAStartup(MAKEWORD(2,2), &wsa);
    SOCKET sock = socket(AF_INET, SOCK_DGRAM, 0);
    sockaddr_in serverAddr = {};
    serverAddr.sin_family = AF_INET;
    serverAddr.sin_addr.s_addr = inet_addr("127.0.0.1");
```

```
    serverAddr.sin_port = htons(9090);
    const char* message = "Hello UDP Server!";
    sendto(sock, message, strlen(message), 0,
           (sockaddr*)&serverAddr, sizeof(serverAddr));
    char buffer[1024];
    sockaddr_in fromAddr;
    int fromLen = sizeof(fromAddr);
    int bytesReceived = recvfrom(sock, buffer, sizeof(buffer),
0,
                                 (sockaddr*)&fromAddr,
&fromLen);
    if (bytesReceived > 0) {
        std::cout << "Echo from server: ";
        std::cout.write(buffer, bytesReceived);
        std::cout << std::endl;
    }
    closesocket(sock);
    WSACleanup();
    return 0;
}
```

With UDP, you're always in charge of handling packet loss, duplicates, or out-of-order arrival if they matter to your app. If reliability or order is essential, you can build those checks too into your message format and logic.

Both the TCP and UDP socket programming bring you close to the network, with a clear mapping between protocol features and code structure. If you have learned this chapter thoroughly, you will find yourself naturally thinking about how connection state, reliability, speed, and packet management align with your application's goals.

Summary

In this chapter, you've learned how internet protocols work, starting with a look at protocol stacks and the differences between TCP and UDP. They explained the mechanics of each protocol, showing how reliable, connection-oriented transfers differ from fast, connectionless communication using real-world examples. We looked at how TCP and UDP segments and datagrams are structured, learned how sockets offer a way for apps to interact with the network, and went through the steps of setting up TCP and UDP servers and clients in C++.

We really went over the best ways to do things, like checking for errors, managing resources well, controlling blocking and timeouts, and making sure the incoming data was secure. We walked away with the skills to build solid, efficient, and secure networked applications, and you got a handle on the patterns that make sure your apps are reliable, easy to maintain, and can handle a lot of traffic.

Chapter 3: Network Interfaces and Addressing

Chapter Overview

In this chapter, you will begin by uncovering how your Windows system sees and manages all network interfaces, from physical Ethernet and Wi-Fi cards to virtual adapters used by VPNs and containers. You will learn why each interface matters, how the OS assigns both IPv4 and IPv6 addresses, and how network addressing structures every communication between devices. You will explore the mechanics of subnetting, moving from reading and writing subnet masks and CIDR notation to actually segmenting networks for organization and security. You will work through detailed, hands-on exercises to configure IP addresses, validate subnets, and diagnose interface assignments using both C++ code and Windows networking tools. With every step, you will tie theory to practice: reading interface lists, scripting checks for address ranges, and understanding how subnets affect reachability and communication paths.

As the chapter progresses, you will build and test your own TCP server and client, reinforcing your understanding by running these programs, sending and receiving data, and applying techniques for resource management and troubleshooting. By the end, you will be able to approach any real Windows network with confidence, designing, deploying, and maintaining robust networked applications, fully aware of how interfaces, addresses, and subnets shape everything your code can do.

Network Interfaces and Addressing

Every networked device you encounter, your laptop, a server in the cloud, or even a smart plug on your desk, has to "join" the network using something called a network interface. Imagine this interface as the digital handshake between your computer and the outside world. The hardware side could be a physical Ethernet port, a Wi-Fi card, a Bluetooth adapter, or even a virtual device created by a VPN or a Docker container. Each of these gives your device a doorway for sending and receiving packets.

To truly understand how data moves between computers, you need to appreciate that a network interface is more than just a port or a cable, it's the active boundary where software, operating system, and physical hardware all meet. Each interface serves as a logical endpoint for communication, exposing a set of technical properties that directly impact how your C++ programs send and receive packets.

Interfaces as Endpoints

At the **Data Link layer** (Layer 2), a network interface represents the unique node for protocols like Ethernet or Wi-Fi. Here, addressing uses the MAC address, hardwired into every network card and globally unique. Every Ethernet frame you send in C++ will be tagged with your NIC's MAC address as source, and the destination's MAC as target.

Step up to the **Network layer** (Layer 3), and each interface is associated with one or more IP addresses, often both IPv4 and IPv6. These addresses are logical and can be reassigned, enabling routing, subnetting, and dynamic configuration. The OS maintains a mapping from interface (hardware) to address (logical) in its routing tables, and your code's binding and packet delivery depend on these mappings.

Most modern systems have several network interfaces: a wired port, a wireless adapter, a loopback interface (`127.0.0.1` or `::1`), and sometimes virtual adapters (for VPNs, VMs, or containers). Each interface may have multiple IP addresses, supporting multi-homing, IPv4/IPv6 dual stack, or multiple VLANs. This is why your C++ server, if bound to **`INADDR_ANY`**, will accept connections on all active IP addresses for every interface, not just one.

Address Assignment and Scope

An interface's addresses can be:

- **Static** (manually configured by admin or script),
- **Dynamic** (assigned by DHCP, SLAAC, or PPP),
- **Link-local** (auto-assigned for IPv6 or Windows APIPA for IPv4, used only within the local segment).

This directly affects how your C++ applications discover peers, advertise themselves, or enforce access policies. For example, if your application needs to communicate across VLANs or subnets, you may have to explicitly enumerate all interfaces and their assigned addresses, not just "localhost."

Each interface, whether real or virtual, comes with:

- **A name** (e.g., "Ethernet 2" or "wlp3s0"),
- **A hardware (MAC) address**,
- **One or more IP addresses** (IPv4, IPv6, link-local, multicast),
- **A netmask or prefix length** (defines local subnet),
- **A status** (up/down, running, enabled/disabled),
- **MTU** (Maximum Transmission Unit, affecting how large each packet can be).

Enumerating Interfaces

To write network-aware applications, you often need to list and inspect all interfaces and their addresses and you can use platform APIs such as **`GetAdaptersAddresses()`** (from IP Helper API) for our system, and if it is Linux, then we use **`getifaddrs()`** (returns a linked list of interfaces and addresses). This lets you, for example, build a network diagnostic tool that shows all interfaces, assigned addresses, their current status (up, down, running), and even details like bandwidth and MTU.

Let us take an example of listing Interfaces in Linux as below:

```
struct ifaddrs *ifaddr, *ifa;
getifaddrs(&ifaddr);
for (ifa = ifaddr; ifa != NULL; ifa = ifa->ifa_next) {
    if (ifa->ifa_addr->sa_family == AF_INET) {
        // Print interface name and address
    }
}
freeifaddrs(ifaddr);
```

This above can detect which interface is "up," which one has a public address, or which should be used for binding or monitoring.

IP Addresses and Subnets

Every device that wants to communicate on a network, whether it's your laptop, a cloud VM, or a sensor node, needs a unique identifier at the **network layer**. This identifier is the **IP address**. The two main versions are IPv4 (the old standby, e.g., **192.168.10.34**) and IPv6 (designed for a much larger address space, e.g., **2001:0db8:85a3::8a2e:0370:7334**).

An IP address isn't just a flat number; it's structured to encode **network identity** and **host identity** within that network. For instance, in IPv4, a subnet mask like **255.255.255.0** (or **/24**) tells you that the first three octets (**192.168.10**) describe the network, and the last octet identifies the host. This split is how routers, switches, and your own OS decide where to deliver each packet, local subnet or out to the wider world.

Without subnetting, the networks would quickly become unmanageable and insecure. **Subnetting** breaks large address ranges into smaller, logical groupings. Each subnet can have its own policies, gateway, and broadcast domain. This allows you to:

- Limit broadcast traffic and collisions.
- Organize devices by function, department, or security zone.
- Assign different routing and firewall rules for each subnet.

In practice, you might see your office's Wi-Fi use **192.168.1.0/24** (devices get **192.168.1.x**), while a guest Wi-Fi lives at **192.168.50.0/24**, even though both plug into the same router. When you configure a device, you always set an IP address, subnet mask (or prefix), gateway, and usually one or more DNS servers.

As you begin to think in subnets, you will find yourself reading and writing CIDR notation fluently, calculating how many hosts fit in a block, or slicing up a **/24** into two **/25**s when you need to segment a lab from production. Modern C++ and network APIs will expect you to parse, validate, and sometimes generate these notations as part of your day-to-day tasks.

Perform Subnetting and IP Configuration

Now, let's get our hands on the real work of subnetting and configuring IPs.

Subnetting by Hand

Let us assume that you're tasked with splitting a company's **192.168.100.0/24** network into four equally-sized subnets. Each subnet will need its own network address, broadcast address, and range for usable hosts, as shown below:

1. The first subnet starts at **192.168.100.0**. The usable addresses go from **.1** to **.62**, while **.0** is reserved as the network address and **.63** is reserved as the broadcast address.
2. The second subnet begins at **192.168.100.64**, with usable addresses from **.65** to **.126**, while **.64** is the network address and **.127** is the broadcast address.
3. The third subnet begins at **192.168.100.128**, with usable addresses from **.129** to **.190**, while **.128** is the network address and **.191** is the broadcast address.
4. The fourth subnet begins at **192.168.100.192**, with usable addresses from **.193** to **.254**, while **.192** is the network address and **.255** is the broadcast address.

You see this logic embedded in firewall rules, DHCP server configuration, and access control policies.

Programmatic Subnetting

Suppose you want to calculate and print all the network addresses for a given **/24** split into **/26** subnets:

```
#include <iostream>
#include <winsock2.h>
void print_subnets(const std::string& base, int new_prefix) {
    uint32_t base_ip = inet_addr(base.c_str());
    int host_bits = 32 - new_prefix;
    int subnet_size = 1 << host_bits;
    for (int i = 0; i < 4; ++i) {
        uint32_t subnet_ip = ntohl(base_ip) + (i *
subnet_size);
```

```
        in_addr subnet_addr;
        subnet_addr.s_addr = htonl(subnet_ip);
        std::cout << "Subnet " << (i + 1) << ": " <<
inet_ntoa(subnet_addr)
                  << "/" << new_prefix << std::endl;
    }
}
int main() {
    print_subnets("192.168.100.0", 26);
    return 0;
}
```

This above snippet reveals the math behind every real-world network plan: each subnet increments the base address by its size, so you can script, validate, or even automate large IP allocations.

You may use PowerShell or Command Prompt to view and set addresses:

```
netsh interface ip set address "Ethernet" static
192.168.100.10 255.255.255.192 192.168.100.1
```

A simple C++ routine for verifying if two IPs are in the same subnet (using mask):

```
bool in_same_subnet(const std::string& ip1, const std::string&
ip2, const std::string& mask) {
    uint32_t addr1 = inet_addr(ip1.c_str());
    uint32_t addr2 = inet_addr(ip2.c_str());
    uint32_t netmask = inet_addr(mask.c_str());
    return (addr1 & netmask) == (addr2 & netmask);
}
```

When you grasp subnetting and IP assignment at this level, across config files, command lines, and C++ code, you're ready to design, automate, and troubleshoot real networks at scale. Each script or service you build will operate with confidence in the network's actual topology, not just in theory.

Create TCP Server and Client

You've already mastered the concepts around the sockets and addressing. Now you can start to write a TCP server and client, compile them with Visual Studio's tools, and see them working on your own Windows machine.

Building TCP Server

You can think of your server as a process waiting for connections. It sits on a port you choose, like 4000, using your network interface's IP or any available address. Each client gets its own socket, so you can handle multiple clients one after another or (later) in parallel.

Following is a simple TCP server sample program:

```
#include <winsock2.h>
#include <iostream>
#pragma comment(lib, "ws2_32.lib")
int main() {
    WSADATA wsa;
    if (WSAStartup(MAKEWORD(2,2), &wsa) != 0) {
        std::cerr << "WSAStartup failed\n";
        return 1;
    }
    SOCKET listenSock = socket(AF_INET, SOCK_STREAM, 0);
    if (listenSock == INVALID_SOCKET) {
        std::cerr << "Socket creation failed\n";
        WSACleanup();
        return 1;
    }
    sockaddr_in serverAddr = {};
    serverAddr.sin_family = AF_INET;
    serverAddr.sin_addr.s_addr = INADDR_ANY; // Listen on all
local IPs
    serverAddr.sin_port = htons(4000);
    if (bind(listenSock, (sockaddr*)&serverAddr,
sizeof(serverAddr)) == SOCKET_ERROR) {
        std::cerr << "Bind failed\n";
```

```
        closesocket(listenSock);
        WSACleanup();
        return 1;
    }
    if (listen(listenSock, SOMAXCONN) == SOCKET_ERROR) {
        std::cerr << "Listen failed\n";
        closesocket(listenSock);
        WSACleanup();
        return 1;
    }
    std::cout << "Server running on port 4000...\n";
    while (true) {
        SOCKET clientSock = accept(listenSock, nullptr,
nullptr);
        if (clientSock == INVALID_SOCKET) continue;
        char buffer[1024] = {0};
        int received = recv(clientSock, buffer,
sizeof(buffer), 0);
        if (received > 0) {
            std::string reply = "Server received: ";
            send(clientSock, reply.c_str(), (int)reply.size(),
0);
            send(clientSock, buffer, received, 0);
        }
        closesocket(clientSock); // Always close
    }
    closesocket(listenSock);
    WSACleanup();
    return 0;
}
```

In order to compile and run, open the "Developer Command Prompt for VS.", then run **cl /EHsc tcp_server.cpp ws2_32.lib**, followed by the output: **tcp_server.exe.** This will give following result:

```
Server running on port 4000...
```

Building TCP Client

Now the client's job is to connect to the server's IP/port, send a message, and read the response. If the server is running on the same machine, you will use **127.0.0.1**.

Following is the TCP Client sample program:

```
#include <winsock2.h>

#include <iostream>

#pragma comment(lib, "ws2_32.lib")

int main() {

    WSADATA wsa;

    if (WSAStartup(MAKEWORD(2,2), &wsa) != 0) {

        std::cerr << "WSAStartup failed\n";

        return 1;

    }

    SOCKET sock = socket(AF_INET, SOCK_STREAM, 0);

    if (sock == INVALID_SOCKET) {

        std::cerr << "Socket creation failed\n";

        WSACleanup();

        return 1;

    }

    sockaddr_in serverAddr = {};

    serverAddr.sin_family = AF_INET;

    serverAddr.sin_addr.s_addr = inet_addr("127.0.0.1");

    serverAddr.sin_port = htons(4000);

    if (connect(sock, (sockaddr*)&serverAddr,
sizeof(serverAddr)) == SOCKET_ERROR) {

        std::cerr << "Connect failed\n";
```

```
        closesocket(sock);
        WSACleanup();
        return 1;
    }
    std::string msg = "Hello from client!";
    send(sock, msg.c_str(), (int)msg.size(), 0);
    char buffer[1024] = {0};
    int received = recv(sock, buffer, sizeof(buffer), 0);
    if (received > 0) {
        std::cout << "Reply: ";
        std::cout.write(buffer, received);
        std::cout << std::endl;
    }
    closesocket(sock);
    WSACleanup();
    return 0;
}
```

After this, run:

```
cl /EHsc tcp_client.cpp ws2_32.lib
```

After this, the server displays connection, receives and echoes data. The client displays:

```
Reply: Server received: Hello from client!Hello from client!
```

TCP/UDP Connections Challenges

Every real network program faces these. Here's how you see and solve them in code:

Partial Send/Receive

The Winsock's **`recv()`** or **`send()`** does not guarantee to process the entire buffer in one call. You must use loops for large messages:

```
int send_all(SOCKET sock, const char* buf, int len) {
    int sent = 0;
```

```
    while (sent < len) {
        int n = send(sock, buf + sent, len - sent, 0);
        if (n == SOCKET_ERROR) return n;
        sent += n;
    }
    return sent;
}
```

Connection Drops

If a client disconnects, **`recv()`** returns 0. On errors, you may get **SOCKET_ERROR**:

```
int n = recv(clientSock, buffer, sizeof(buffer), 0);
if (n == 0) {
    std::cout << "Connection closed by client\n";
} else if (n == SOCKET_ERROR) {
    std::cerr << "Recv failed: " << WSAGetLastError() << "\n";
}
```

Timeouts

Avoid hanging forever by setting socket timeouts:

```
int timeout = 3000; // milliseconds
setsockopt(clientSock, SOL_SOCKET, SO_RCVTIMEO,
(char*)&timeout, sizeof(timeout));
```

If no data is received within 3 seconds, **`recv()`** fails and you can log or clean up.

UDP Loss and Out-of-Order Handling

If you move to UDP, packets can be lost or arrive out of order. Here's a basic sequence number approach for UDP:

Sender

```
uint32_t seq = 1;
memcpy(buffer, &seq, sizeof(seq));
// ... fill rest ...
```

```
sendto(sock, buffer, sizeof(buffer), 0, (sockaddr*)&addr, sizeof(addr));
```

Receiver

```
uint32_t rseq = 0;
memcpy(&rseq, buffer, sizeof(rseq));
if (rseq != expected_seq) {
    std::cout << "Packet out of order or lost! Expected: " << expected_seq << " Got: " << rseq << std::endl;
}
expected_seq = rseq + 1;
```

Apart from the above ones, always clean up sockets with **`closesocket()`** and call **`WSACleanup()`** at the end of your program, no matter the path taken. Every challenge here is a real, recurring issue for Windows C++ network developers.

Summary

Throughout this chapter, you gained a working knowledge of network interfaces and how addressing operates on modern Windows systems. You discovered that every network device, whether physical or virtual, is represented as a network interface, each with its own technical properties such as MAC address, IP address, operational state, and assignment method. You learned how the OS manages multiple interfaces and assigns IP addresses, both IPv4 and IPv6, depending on configuration and network needs.

The concept of subnetting was explored in depth, showing how logical partitioning of address spaces provides organization, isolation, and scalability. You saw how to read and interpret subnet masks and CIDR notation, calculate network and broadcast addresses, and use this knowledge to segment networks practically. Building on this, you developed hands-on C++ programs to enumerate interfaces, verify IP configurations, and implement real TCP servers and clients, including full code and exact steps to execute and troubleshoot these programs on Windows. Finally, you encountered the real-world challenges of partial reads and writes, handling timeouts, managing dropped connections, and robust resource cleanup, learning how to identify and mitigate these issues in your own network applications.

CHAPTER 4: APPLICATION LAYER PROTOCOLS

Chapter Overview

In this chapter, you'll start exploring the protocols and services at the top of the networking stack. These are the ones that control how users and systems interact with each other across the internet. First, you'll get to understand the application layer and its role in things like browsing, file sharing, and communications. You'll dive into the ins and outs of HTTP and HTTPS, learning how requests are structured and why secure communication is a must for today's web.

We're going to break down FTP for you so you can learn how to move files manually and how to automate file transfers securely and efficiently. You'll get to dive into the world of email, learning the ropes of sending with SMTP and handling your inbox with IMAP. And you'll see the nitty-gritty that makes these systems work well together and keep things reliable. You'll learn how DNS is crucial for connecting names and addresses, and you'll get hands-on experience with using and troubleshooting it for your own apps. It'll also teach you how to deal with errors in a graceful way and how to debug and recover across all major application layer protocols. By the time you're done, you'll be ready to build, automate, and maintain complex applications that depend on a solid understanding of how these essential protocols function in practice.

Application Layer

What if you're using a web browser to check your email, upload a file to a remote server, or join a video meeting? All of these experiences are powered by protocols that operate at the Application Layer. If you think of the networking stack as a ladder, the Application Layer is like the top rung. That's where the software you use interacts with the network underneath. It's where protocols finally stop worrying about the little details of packet delivery and start enabling real-world tasks like web browsing, email, file transfer, messaging, and streaming.

In both the OSI and TCP/IP models, the Application Layer is where processes and users connect with network services. While lower layers (Transport, Network, Data Link) handle how data moves from point A to point B, the Application Layer defines what that data means. It sets the rules for interaction, authentication, data formatting, and how information is requested, sent, and presented to users. The protocols like **HTTP** (web browsing), **HTTPS** (secure web), **FTP** (file transfer), **SMTP/IMAP** (email), and **DNS** (domain name lookup) live here. Each protocol provides a standard way for software to speak to remote systems, no matter the programming language or platform. For instance, when you fetch a webpage, your browser and the web server both "speak" HTTP, exchanging requests and responses that both sides know how to interpret.

As a C++ developer, your programs can use these protocols directly, making your applications act as clients (consuming services) or servers (providing services). Most of the Application Layer protocols are text-based and relatively human-readable, so you can test them with simple tools (like **`telnet`**, **`curl`**, or your own C++ socket code) before you even build a user interface. You will find that some protocols (like HTTP, SMTP) work best over TCP for reliability, while others (like DNS) may use both TCP and UDP, depending on the request. Application Layer protocols are typically designed to be independent of lower network details. As long as your code can open a socket and send/receive data, you can implement nearly any protocol.

In fact, the Application Layer protocols makes you far more effective at:

- Debugging and tracing data flows.
- Building custom clients or services.
- Troubleshooting why a web request or upload fails.
- Securing user data.

Each of the protocol comes with its own rules, expected headers or commands, and sometimes security implications. As you progress, you will see how protocols like HTTP and HTTPS make it easy to fetch or post data to a server, while others like SMTP/IMAP provide ways to automate or monitor email flows. You will get to build and test programs that talk directly to real-world servers, send web requests, upload files, query DNS, and even automate email, all in C++. Every protocol you learn is a new tool you can apply in your own projects or integrate into larger systems, giving you a real edge as a networking developer.

HTTP and HTTPS Deep Dive

If you consider about every website you visit, every online search, every API call, almost all are powered by HTTP or its secure sibling, HTTPS. These protocols define how browsers, mobile apps, IoT devices, and cloud services communicate on the internet.

What is HTTP?

HTTP (HyperText Transfer Protocol) is a text-based, stateless protocol that lets clients (like browsers) and servers (like websites or APIs) exchange requests and responses. Each transaction starts with the client opening a connection to a server (usually on port 80 for HTTP), sending a request line (such as **`GET /index.html HTTP/1.1`**), and then the server responds with status, headers, and optional data.

A single HTTP request/response looks like this:

```
GET /index.html HTTP/1.1
Host: gitforgits.com
User-Agent: MyClient/1.0
HTTP/1.1 200 OK
Content-Type: text/html
<html> ... </html>
```

HTTP supports several methods, **`GET`**, **`POST`**, **`PUT`**, **`DELETE`**, etc., each with a specific purpose. **`GET`** retrieves data, **`POST`** submits data (like a form), **`DELETE`** removes a resource, and so on.

HTTP/1.1 remains widely used, but HTTP/2 and HTTP/3 introduce multiplexing and improved performance.

Security with HTTPS

HTTP traffic is plain text. Anyone who can sniff the network can read the content, including sensitive data. **HTTPS** (HTTP Secure) solves this by running HTTP inside a secure tunnel using **TLS (Transport Layer Security)**. With HTTPS (typically on port 443), all headers, data, cookies, and credentials are encrypted before leaving your machine.

Today, HTTPS is considered mandatory for nearly all public websites and APIs. Browsers flag sites as "insecure" without it. Certificates (issued by trusted authorities) prove a site's identity, and the TLS handshake ensures privacy and data integrity.

HTTP and HTTPS Requests with Boost Beast

The Boost Beast is a modern C++ library for both HTTP and WebSocket protocols. Here's how you can make HTTP and HTTPS requests directly from your C++ application, handling all the protocol details for you.

HTTP GET Program

Following is an HTTP GET example that connects to a remote server (such as **`gitforgits.com`**), sends a GET request, and prints the response:

```
#include <boost/beast/core.hpp>
#include <boost/beast/http.hpp>
#include <boost/asio/connect.hpp>
#include <boost/asio/ip/tcp.hpp>
#include <iostream>
namespace http = boost::beast::http;
namespace net = boost::asio;
using tcp = net::ip::tcp;
int main() {
    try {
        auto const host = "gitforgits.com";
        auto const port = "80";
        auto const target = "/index.html";
```

```
        int version = 11;
        net::io_context ioc;
        tcp::resolver resolver(ioc);
        auto const results = resolver.resolve(host, port);
        tcp::socket socket(ioc);
        net::connect(socket, results.begin(), results.end());
        http::request<http::string_body> req{http::verb::get,
target, version};
        req.set(http::field::host, host);
        req.set(http::field::user_agent, "Custom-Client/1.0");
        http::write(socket, req);
        boost::beast::flat_buffer buffer;
        http::response<http::dynamic_body> res;
        http::read(socket, buffer, res);
        std::cout << res << std::endl;
        socket.shutdown(tcp::socket::shutdown_both);
    }
    catch (std::exception const& e) {
        std::cerr << "Error: " << e.what() << std::endl;
        return 1;
    }
    return 0;
}
```

In the above, you can customize the **`target`**, method, or headers to perform API requests, submit forms, or scrape data. The response object gives you full access to headers, status, and body.

HTTPS GET Program

And for HTTPS, the only major difference is the need to perform a TLS handshake using Boost.Asio's SSL support, and you will also need OpenSSL installed and linked in our windows system:

```
#include <boost/asio.hpp>
#include <boost/asio/ssl.hpp>
#include <boost/beast/http.hpp>
#include <iostream>
namespace http = boost::beast::http;
namespace net = boost::asio;
namespace ssl = net::ssl;
using tcp = net::ip::tcp;
int main() {
    try {
        auto const host = "gitforgits.com";
        auto const port = "443";
        auto const target = "/";
        int version = 11;
        net::io_context ioc;
        ssl::context ctx{ssl::context::tlsv12_client};
        ctx.set_default_verify_paths();
        tcp::resolver resolver{ioc};
        auto const results = resolver.resolve(host, port);
        ssl::stream<tcp::socket> stream{ioc, ctx};
        net::connect(stream.next_layer(), results.begin(),
results.end());
        stream.handshake(ssl::stream_base::client);
        http::request<http::string_body> req{http::verb::get,
target, version};
        req.set(http::field::host, host);
        req.set(http::field::user_agent, "Custom-Client/1.0");
        http::write(stream, req);
        boost::beast::flat_buffer buffer;
        http::response<http::dynamic_body> res;
```

```
        http::read(stream, buffer, res);
        std::cout << res << std::endl;
        stream.shutdown();
    }
    catch (std::exception const& e) {
        std::cerr << "Error: " << e.what() << std::endl;
        return 1;
    }
    return 0;
}
```

After this, you can extend this for POST, custom headers, handling cookies, or integrating with APIs. When targeting real production servers, set **`ctx.set_verify_mode(ssl::verify_peer)`**`;` and configure certificate validation for real security.

With these building blocks, you can automate downloads, build web clients, test APIs, or even write your own HTTP server in C++. Your applications can interact with nearly any web service or automate any web-facing workflow.

FTP Deep Dive

The FTP (File Transfer Protocol) is one of the oldest, simplest ways to move files between computers over a TCP network. It uses two separate channels, one is the **Control Channel** which is always on TCP port 21, for commands (**`USER`**, **`PASS`**, **`LIST`**, **`STOR`**, etc.); and the other is **Data Channel** which is dynamically opened for each transfer. The FTP commands are text-based, and the server responds with numeric codes (**`220 Welcome`**, **`530 Login incorrect`**, **`226 Transfer complete`**). FTP is stateful, the connection persists for your session.

Using and Automating FTP

First, open the command prompt, and then type:

```
ftp ftp.dlptest.com
```

After this, login with provided test credentials and try the following commands:

- **`ls`** to list files
- **`get sample.txt`** to download
- **`put mydata.txt`** to upload

- **delete file.txt** to remove
- **bye** or **quit** to exit

If the data channel fails (**425** error), then you need to type **passive** to switch mode.

Automating FTP with WinINet

Now here, you can connect, download, and upload using the pure Windows APIs, and no such cross-platform code or third-party binaries are needed.

```
#include <windows.h>

#include <wininet.h>

#include <iostream>

int main() {

    HINTERNET hInternet = InternetOpen(L"FTPApp",
INTERNET_OPEN_TYPE_DIRECT, NULL, NULL, 0);

    HINTERNET hFtpSession = InternetConnect(hInternet,
L"ftp.dlptest.com", INTERNET_DEFAULT_FTP_PORT,

                                            L"dlpuser",
L"rNrKYTX9g7z3RgJRmxWuGHbeu", INTERNET_SERVICE_FTP, 0, 0);

    // List remote files

    WIN32_FIND_DATA findData;

    HINTERNET hFind = FtpFindFirstFile(hFtpSession, NULL,
&findData, 0, 0);

    if (hFind) {

        do {

            std::wcout << findData.cFileName << std::endl;

        } while (InternetFindNextFile(hFind, &findData));

        InternetCloseHandle(hFind);

    }

    // Download a file

    if (FtpGetFile(hFtpSession, L"sample.txt",
L"sample_downloaded.txt", FALSE, FILE_ATTRIBUTE_NORMAL,
FTP_TRANSFER_TYPE_BINARY, 0))

        std::cout << "Download successful." << std::endl;
```

```
    // Upload a file
    if (FtpPutFile(hFtpSession, L"mydata.txt",
L"uploaded_by_cpp.txt", FTP_TRANSFER_TYPE_BINARY, 0))
        std::cout << "Upload successful." << std::endl;
    InternetCloseHandle(hFtpSession);
    InternetCloseHandle(hInternet);
    return 0;
}
```

After running the above, it initializes an FTP session, authenticates, and lists directory contents. It downloads and uploads files, each time opening a new data channel. These steps lets you automate regular backups, deployment, or integration with legacy systems where FTP is still used. You will also see why so many systems have shifted to SFTP or FTPS, security and firewall issues are real.

SMTP & IMAP Deep Dive

SMTP Overview

The SMTP (Simple Mail Transfer Protocol) is designed to transmit email reliably between mail clients and servers over TCP, usually on port 25, 587, or 465 (TLS/SSL). It's a text-based, command/response protocol.

Following is a typical SMTP workflow:

1. Connect to the server.
2. Authenticate it.
3. Then, send the envelope: **MAIL FROM**, **RCPT TO**.
4. After this, Send the message with **DATA** and end with a single period on its own line.
5. And then finally disconnect.

The SMTPs, like FTP, are insecure without TLS and almost all servers require SSL and strong authentication.

Sending Email using 'libcurl'

To get going, get your credentials ready (that's your App password for Gmail/Outlook). Then write some C++ code, ;like the following one to send the email:

```
#include <curl/curl.h>
```

```
int main() {
    CURL* curl = curl_easy_init();
    if (curl) {
        struct curl_slist* rcpts = nullptr;
        rcpts = curl_slist_append(rcpts, "to@domain.com");
        curl_easy_setopt(curl, CURLOPT_URL,
"smtp://smtp.gmail.com:587");
        curl_easy_setopt(curl, CURLOPT_MAIL_FROM,
"from@gmail.com");
        curl_easy_setopt(curl, CURLOPT_MAIL_RCPT, rcpts);
        curl_easy_setopt(curl, CURLOPT_USERNAME,
"from@gmail.com");
        curl_easy_setopt(curl, CURLOPT_PASSWORD,
"your_app_password");
        curl_easy_setopt(curl, CURLOPT_USE_SSL,
(long)CURLUSESSL_ALL);
        const char* msg = "To: to@domain.com\r\nFrom:
from@gmail.com\r\nSubject: Test\r\n\r\nHello from C++.\r\n";
        curl_easy_setopt(curl, CURLOPT_READFUNCTION, NULL);
        curl_easy_setopt(curl, CURLOPT_READDATA, (void*)msg);
        curl_easy_setopt(curl, CURLOPT_UPLOAD, 1L);
        CURLcode res = curl_easy_perform(curl);
        if (res != CURLE_OK)
            std::cout << curl_easy_strerror(res) << std::endl;
        curl_slist_free_all(rcpts);
        curl_easy_cleanup(curl);
    }
    return 0;
}
```

After this, then you built it:

```
cl /EHsc yourfile.cpp /I"path\to\curl\include" /link
/LIBPATH:"path\to\curl\lib" libcurl.lib
```

In the above, if credentials are correct, the mail is sent. If not, you will see error codes (535 = bad login, 530 = auth required, 550 = relay denied).

IMAP Overview

The IMAPs (Internet Message Access Protocol) allows clients to manage and read emails on the server, usually over port 143 (plain) or 993 (SSL/TLS).

The ussal orkflow of an IMAP is as below, which is more or same as SMTP:

- Here also, you authenticate to the IMAP server.
- Then, select a mailbox (e.g., INBOX).
- We then fetch message headers, bodies, or attachments using commands like **FETCH**, **SEARCH**, etc.
- And, after this, we then mark messages read, unread, or deleted as needed.

Reading Mail using 'libcurl'

The code to list the latest email is as below:

```
#include <curl/curl.h>

#include <iostream>

size_t print_data(void* ptr, size_t size, size_t nmemb, void*)
{

    std::cout.write((char*)ptr, size * nmemb);

    return size * nmemb;

}

int main() {

    CURL* curl = curl_easy_init();

    if (curl) {

        curl_easy_setopt(curl, CURLOPT_URL,
"imaps://imap.gmail.com/INBOX");

        curl_easy_setopt(curl, CURLOPT_USERNAME,
"your@gmail.com");

        curl_easy_setopt(curl, CURLOPT_PASSWORD,
"your_app_password");
```

```
        curl_easy_setopt(curl, CURLOPT_WRITEFUNCTION,
print_data);
        CURLcode res = curl_easy_perform(curl);
        if (res != CURLE_OK)
            std::cout << curl_easy_strerror(res) << std::endl;
        curl_easy_cleanup(curl);
    }
    return 0;
}
```

The raw server response includes headers, message status, and content.

For full-featured mail processing, we then have to parse these responses ormaybe to use an advanced library like VMime, or the POCO.

DNS Deep Dive

The Domain Name System (DNS) is the "phonebook" of the internet. While computers use IP addresses to route data, humans prefer memorable domain names like **`www.microsoft.com`**. Every time you access a website, send an email, or connect to a remote host, your system must resolve that domain to an IP address, a process known as "DNS lookup." Without DNS, every connection would require raw IPs.

The DNS operates as a distributed, hierarchical system. Our request travels from local cache to DNS resolver (often provided by your ISP or set manually), then up to root servers, TLD servers (like **`.com`** or **`.net`**), and finally to authoritative servers for the target domain. In this whole process, every step caches the answer for speed and efficiency.

The DNS has following record types:

- **A** Maps domain to IPv4 address.
- **AAAA** Maps domain to IPv6.
- **CNAME** is an Alias/redirects to another domain.
- **MX** is the mail server for the domain.
- **TXT** is an arbitrary text, often for verification.

The DNS operates over both UDP and TCP (port 53), with UDP used for most lookups and TCP for larger or more secure exchanges.

Manual DNS Lookup

To begin with, we will first type:

```
nslookup www.gitforgits.com
```

Here, you will see:

```
Name:    www.gitforgits.com
Address: 93.184.216.34
```

Now here, we will try to look up the mail servers:

```
nslookup -type=mx gmail.com
```

After this, you will see all MX records, showing Google's mail servers.

Programmatic DNS Lookup

The ***Winsock*** provides a simple way: **getaddrinfo**. And, this call is not just for DNS, but for all address resolution, including local and remote hosts, IPv4 and IPv6, and even service ports.

```
#include <winsock2.h>
#include <ws2tcpip.h>
#include <iostream>
#pragma comment(lib, "ws2_32.lib")
int main() {
    WSADATA wsa;
    WSAStartup(MAKEWORD(2,2), &wsa);
    addrinfo hints = {}, *res = nullptr;
    hints.ai_family = AF_UNSPEC; // Both IPv4 and IPv6
    hints.ai_socktype = SOCK_STREAM;
    int err = getaddrinfo("www.microsoft.com", nullptr,
&hints, &res);
    if (err == 0) {
        for (addrinfo* p = res; p != nullptr; p = p->ai_next)
{
            char ipstr[INET6_ADDRSTRLEN] = {0};
            void* addr = nullptr;
```

```
            if (p->ai_family == AF_INET) {
                sockaddr_in* ipv4 = (sockaddr_in*)p->ai_addr;
                addr = &(ipv4->sin_addr);
            } else if (p->ai_family == AF_INET6) {
                sockaddr_in6* ipv6 = (sockaddr_in6*)p-
>ai_addr;
                addr = &(ipv6->sin6_addr);
            }
            inet_ntop(p->ai_family, addr, ipstr,
sizeof(ipstr));
            std::cout << "IP: " << ipstr << std::endl;
        }
        freeaddrinfo(res);
    } else {
        std::cerr << "DNS resolution failed: " <<
gai_strerrorA(err) << std::endl;
    }
    WSACleanup();
    return 0;
}
```

Whiel doing this, if you get **WSAHOST_NOT_FOUND**, then you must check typos or your network connection. And, if the result is empty, then the domain has no A/AAAA records.

Basically, all protocols (like HTTP, FTP, SMTP and so on) need DNS to figure out what a hostname is. If you get your DNS lookups right, you'll be able to connect in no time. But if they're not, you'll be in for a rude awakening. It's also important to be aware of DNS poisoning or hijacking, as this can redirect connections to malicious servers.

Error Handling in Socket Programming

There are a few things that can cause errors when you're working with sockets and protocols. Things like network conditions, remote systems, user input, or even bugs in your code can all trigger errors. You've got to check every network call and be ready to deal with all sorts of error codes. When it comes to Windows, pretty much every error can be traced back to either a Winsock error code (for sockets) or a system error (for WinINet, libcurl, etc.).

Following are the typical sources of error:

- DNS failures (name not found, no response)
- Connection errors (timeout, refused, unreachable)
- Protocol errors (unexpected reply, authentication failure)
- Data errors (partial read, unexpected disconnect)

Error Handling by Protocol

DNS (getaddrinfo, nslookup)

With DNS, for example, every query through **getaddrinfo** returns an integer. A zero means "all good," but any other value is an error. Instead of guessing, you should always convert that error code into human words with a function like **gai_strerror**.

It is also wise to make sure the domain name you are passing is well-formed—things like overly long labels or illegal characters can be caught before the request even leaves your program. If the resolver tells you the problem is temporary (such as a transient failure), you can try again with a short pause before each attempt, rather than hammering the system endlessly.

FTP (WinINet, libcurl)

When moving into FTP, the landscape changes. Here, every API call gives you a status. If you're using WinINet, you look at **GetLastError** to see what went wrong. The libcurl helps to translate the code with **curl_easy_strerror**. The FTP server itself often replies with its own numeric messages. A 530 means the login is bad, 550 means the file doesn't exist, 553 is a permissions issue, and 425 tells you the data channel couldn't be opened. If you notice a pattern of repeated failures, the smart move is to reset the session or try passive mode, which tends to work better through firewalls.

SMTP & IMAP (libcurl)

For SMTP and IMAP, you may encounter a similar pattern since libcurl is often the library of choice. So here, when a mail send or fetch fails, the call returns a **CURLcode**. Again, you should translate this to something readable with **curl_easy_strerror**. But beyond that, you need to respect the mail server's language:

- 535 means login failed,
- 530 says authentication is required, and
- 550 indicates the recipient mailbox can't be used.

On the IMAP side, you might see outright connection refusals, missing mailboxes, or SSL issues.

Before even attempting to send mail, validate your recipient addresses and message structure so you don't trip server-side errors that could have been caught locally.

HTTPS (libcurl, Boost.Beast)

The HTTPS adds another layer of complexity. Most failures here come from SSL or TLS. Certificates may be expired, the hostname might not match, or the certificate might be self-signed without a trusted authority. There are libraries like libcurl or Boost.Beast that will hand you a failure code, but the important step is logging these details with as much clarity as possible. You must know that an expired certificate needs a very different remedy than a hostname mismatch, and your program should never silently ignore certificate problems—either guide the operator to install trusted CAs or clearly state why the connection cannot proceed.

General Socket Programming

Finally, at the raw socket level, the principles remain consistent: every call that returns a socket, sends, receives, or connects can fail. Windows will hand you an error code through WSAGetLastError; Unix-like systems will fill errno. When you see timeouts, you can handle them by retrying with a backoff policy. When recv returns zero, that means the connection is closed, and you should treat it as the remote peer hanging up.

Sample Program: Robust DNS and Socket Handling

Following is a ready sample program that ensures to have a strong and robust DNS:

```
int err = getaddrinfo("nonexistent.gitforgits.com", nullptr, &hints, &res);

if (err != 0) {

    std::cerr << "DNS lookup failed: " << gai_strerrorA(err) << std::endl;

    return 1; // or retry after a delay

}

SOCKET s = socket(AF_INET, SOCK_STREAM, 0);

if (s == INVALID_SOCKET) {

    std::cerr << "Socket creation failed: " << WSAGetLastError() << std::endl;

    freeaddrinfo(res);

    return 1;

}
```

```
if (connect(s, res->ai_addr, (int)res->ai_addrlen) ==
SOCKET_ERROR) {
    std::cerr << "Connect failed: " << WSAGetLastError() <<
std::endl;
    closesocket(s);
    freeaddrinfo(res);
    return 1;
}
```

In the above program, we have seen a pattern of **check, log, handle, and recover**. This pattern is at the heart of professional network programming, no matter which protocol you're building or using.

Summary

During this chapter, you had a look at the depth and variety of application layer protocols that make modern networking possible. So, you learned how the application layer is at the top of the network stack. You got to grips with how HTTP and HTTPS actually work, from the way requests and responses are structured to why encryption and certificate validation are needed for secure communication. You did a hands-on session with FTP, learning to transfer files between systems, both manually and using automated scripts, and got to grips with the importance of secure options for sensitive data. We broke down email protocols like SMTP and IMAP so you could understand how emails are sent and how inboxes are accessed and managed.

You learned that the DNS is basically the service that translates human-friendly domain names into IP addresses, which makes it possible to use user-friendly domains for all types of connections. You also practised resolving domains programmatically and diagnosing issues using built-in Windows tools. At last, you've been trained to spot, deal with and sort out any problems with all these protocols, making sure your apps stay strong and reliable, even when there are network issues, authentication failures or errors specific to the protocol.

CHAPTER 5: VPNs

Chapter Overview

This chapter will provide you with a clear, practical understanding of VPNs, showing you how they enable secure, private communication across even the most public networks. You will start by exploring the fundamental principles that underpin VPNs and the business scenarios that render these technologies indispensable for contemporary organisations.

As you progress, you will learn the differences between site-to-site and remote access VPNs, and understand why each is necessary and how they are implemented in practice. You will also be introduced to the protocols that power VPNs, such as IPsec, OpenVPN and WireGuard which gives you the technical insight needed to evaluate and select the right solution for your projects. You will walk through the process of installing OpenVPN on Windows, generating and managing the cryptographic keys and certificates required for secure communication, and configuring server and client systems to establish robust, encrypted tunnels. You'll learn all about real-world troubleshooting and automation tips to handle and resolve any issue that might come up, whether you're setting up a secure branch office link or enabling remote access for a global workforce. By the end of the chapter, you will have acquired the necessary skills and practical experience to deploy, manage and automate VPN solutions with confidence in any environment.

Introduction to Virtual Private Networks

In today's connected world, the challenge of keeping network activity private and secure is faced by every organisation and many individuals, especially when public networks are used or remote resources are accessed. The solution is Virtual Private Networks (VPNs). A VPN creates a secure, encrypted tunnel across the open internet. When your device connects to the internet via a VPN, all your network traffic is encrypted, meaning outsiders, hackers and even your internet service provider cannot see or tamper with the content of your communications.

Say you're working from a café and using the open Wi-Fi. Without a VPN, your network traffic would be visible to anyone nearby with basic sniffing tools. Once a connection has been established through a VPN client, every byte, email, code, file, or credential is transported inside an encrypted tunnel, ensuring protection from prying eyes. On the corporate side, the possibility of remote employees, branch offices, or contractors connecting into the main network as if they were inside the company's firewall is made possible by VPNs, even when working from distant locations.

The typical VPN solution consists of a few essential components:

- **VPN Client** on your device, managing encryption/decryption and the connection itself
- **VPN Server or Gateway**, acting as the endpoint and enforcing security rules
- **The Encrypted Tunnel**, which protects the data in transit
- **Security Protocols** (such as IPsec, SSL/TLS, WireGuard, OpenVPN) which define how data is encrypted and authenticated

The VPNs also enable content unblocking and geolocation masking. For example, if your organization has offices in different countries or you need to access resources as if you're in a different region, VPNs can reroute your traffic through a remote server, giving your device a virtual presence there. You can experience this by connecting to a VPN endpoint in another country and immediately seeing region-specific websites, search results, or even different streaming libraries.

As more companies adopt hybrid and remote work, the VPNs become foundational for secure remote access, regulatory compliance (in fields like healthcare and finance), and scalable network expansion. The Modern VPNs are increasingly simple to deploy, manage, and automate, making them essential for every professional who manages or develops networked applications, especially as data privacy regulations grow stricter each year.

Types of VPN

We must remember thart the VPNs are not one-size-fits-all. There are several types, each designed for specific connectivity needs and business environments. As a professional, you will want to recognize which type matches your use case, whether that's secure access for remote employees, connecting multiple office sites, or working with external vendors.

Site-to-Site VPN

When an organization has multiple offices or facilities in different geographic locations, it needs a way to securely bridge these networks over the internet. A **Site-to-Site VPN** achieves this by linking entire networks through VPN gateways, routers, firewalls, or dedicated devices. There are two primary flavors:

- The **Intranet-based Site-to-Site VPNs** connect multiple company locations, so users in one office can access shared drives, printers, or internal applications at another location as if on the same LAN.
- And, the **Extranet-based Site-to-Site VPNs** link a company with external partners or vendors. In this case, the connection is tightly controlled so only certain resources are shared.

Every site-to-site VPN relies on pre-configured tunnels and encryption policies. The end user doesn't have to launch or log into anything, the connection is always on, handled entirely by network infrastructure.

Remote Access VPN

For organizations with mobile users, telecommuters, or field engineers, a **Remote Access VPN** is the standard solution. Each user runs a VPN client on their laptop, phone, or tablet. The client establishes an encrypted connection to a corporate VPN gateway, authenticates, and joins the network. The encrypted tunnel protects their session, even when using insecure public Wi-Fi. The Remote Access VPNs can be further divided as:

- **IPsec-based** which offers robust, network-level security, often used in enterprise environments. Requires installation and setup of a VPN client.
- And, the **SSL VPN** which utilizes the SSL or TLS, often accessible via web browsers, being very popular for BYODand contractor access, as well as small and medium-sized businesses.

VPN Protocols

The VPN protocols are the engines that power every secure tunnel. Each protocol defines how your data is encrypted, authenticated, and transmitted between endpoints. As a C++ networking professional or IT architect, understanding the strengths, weaknesses, and implementation details of major VPN protocols will help you select, troubleshoot, and even script the best-fit solution for each scenario.

Popular Protocols In-use

- **PPTP (Point-to-Point Tunneling Protocol)**

  Once popular due to its simplicity and ease of setup, PPTP is now considered obsolete and insecure. Its encryption (MS-CHAPv2) is vulnerable to attacks. Today, it's rarely recommended, and you should migrate any existing PPTP connections to a stronger protocol.

- **L2TP/IPsec (Layer 2 Tunneling Protocol with IPsec)**

  The L2TP itself provides no encryption, so it's nearly always paired with IPsec, which offers robust encryption and authentication. This combination is widely supported by operating systems and network hardware. It supports NAT traversal and can run in either transport or tunnel mode. Setup can be more complex due to key management and firewall configuration.

- **OpenVPN**

  The OpenVPN is a highly flexible, open-source VPN solution that uses SSL/TLS for key exchange and supports a variety of encryption algorithms (AES, Blowfish, ChaCha20, etc.). It's renowned for its reliability and ability to work in almost any network environment, including those with restrictive firewalls. OpenVPN runs on both TCP and UDP ports and allows for advanced configurations such as site-to-site, remote access, and bridging. Its configuration files are text-based and highly scriptable.

- **IKEv2/IPsec (Internet Key Exchange version 2)**

  The IKEv2 is valued for its speed, stability, and excellent support for mobile devices that frequently change networks (such as switching from Wi-Fi to 4G). It offers strong security with modern encryption and is natively supported on Windows, iOS, and many other platforms.

- **WireGuard**

  The WireGuard is a modern, minimalist VPN protocol that is quickly gaining favor for its simple design, fast performance, and cutting-edge cryptography. Its configuration is extremely lightweight (a few lines per peer), making it easy to deploy, audit, and manage. WireGuard operates over UDP and is now integrated into the Linux kernel and supported by Windows, macOS, and mobile devices.

- **SSL VPN**

  The SSL VPNs leverage the same technology as HTTPS (SSL/TLS) and are often delivered via web browsers or lightweight clients. They excel at enabling remote access for BYOD environments and guest devices with minimal configuration.

Now here, whatever protocol you choose for scripting or automating VPN connections will determine how you manage keys, certificates, authentication and error handling. For most new deployments, OpenVPN or WireGuard offers the optimal combination of security, manageability and cross-platform support.

Implementing Site-to-Site VPN

A site-to-site VPN is used to connect the whole network, normally for company offices or data centres, so users at both locations can communicate securely as if they're all on the same physical network. So, as an engineer or administrator, you might be the one who's responsible for planning, configuring, or automating these links. In a big environment, VPN is often used together with central authentication (like RADIUS or LDAP), automated key rotation, and 24/7 monitoring.

Let's say you've got two offices, A and B. Each one has a Windows machine that can act as a VPN endpoint. The idea is to connect these offices securely so each network can reach the other as if they were on the same LAN.

Generate Certificates and Keys

The good thing about OpenVPN is that it has got **easy-rsa** scripts to make it a simple process. To start with, go to the OpenVPN directory and then **easy-rsa**.

```
cd "C:\Program Files\OpenVPN\easy-rsa"

EasyRSA-Start.bat
```

Then, we initialize the Public Key Infrastructure (PKI):

```
./easyrsa init-pki
```

```
./easyrsa build-ca
```

After this, we then generate the server certificate/key:

```
./easyrsa gen-req serverA nopass
./easyrsa sign-req server serverA
```

Similarly, we then generate the client certificate/key:

```
./easyrsa gen-req clientB nopass
./easyrsa sign-req client clientB
```

Next, we then generate Diffie-Hellman parameters and TLS key:

```
./easyrsa gen-dh
openvpn --genkey --secret ta.key
```

We then copy all keys and certificates to appropriate folders (server files to Office A, client files to Office B).

Write Server and Client Config Files

We now work upon the server config as following (Office A, **server.ovpn**):

```
port 1194
proto udp
dev tun
ca ca.crt
cert serverA.crt
key serverA.key
dh dh.pem
server 10.8.0.0 255.255.255.0
ifconfig-pool-persist ipp.txt
keepalive 10 120
tls-auth ta.key 0
cipher AES-256-CBC
persist-key
persist-tun
status openvpn-status.log
```

```
verb 3
```

Also, we then work upon the client config (Office B, **client.ovpn**):

```
client
dev tun
proto udp
remote [SERVER_PUBLIC_IP] 1194
resolv-retry infinite
nobind
persist-key
persist-tun
ca ca.crt
cert clientB.crt
key clientB.key
tls-auth ta.key 1
cipher AES-256-CBC
verb 3
```

Now here, do not forget to replace the **[SERVER_PUBLIC_IP]** with the public IP of Office A.

Start OpenVPN

To do this,

- First, place each config file and its associated certificates/keys in the OpenVPN **config** folder.
- Then, right-click the OpenVPN GUI and "Run as Administrator."
- After this, in the GUI, select your **.ovpn** config and click "Connect."

Tunnel Testing

To do this, first **ping 10.8.0.1** from the client side, and then **ping 10.8.0.x** from the server side (where **x** is the assigned IP).

After this, you should see successful pings, indicating the tunnel is active.

Route Traffic between Networks

The next step is to edit the configs to add push routes, which should allow each LAN to reach the other.

Then on the server, add:

```
push "route 192.168.10.0 255.255.255.0"
```

Similarly on the client-side, you can set up corresponding routes if needed.

Automating Connection Checks

You can use a basic script to check that your VPN is working properly by pinging the remote endpoint and restarting the service if it needs to be fixed.

```
#include <Windows.h>
#include <iostream>
#include <string>
#include <cstdlib>
int main() {
    int result = system("ping -n 2 10.8.0.1");
    if (result != 0) {
        std::cout << "VPN tunnel is down. Attempting
restart..." << std::endl;
        system("net stop OpenVPNService");
        Sleep(2000);
        system("net start OpenVPNService");
    } else {
        std::cout << "VPN tunnel is healthy." << std::endl;
    }
    return 0;
}
```

This above handy step-by-step flow will set you up with OpenVPN on Windows, let you generate and manage certificates, configure secure tunnels, verify connectivity and even script basic monitoring. You'll get a great practical VPN experience that'll really stand out in any networking or development role.

Implementing Remote Access VPN

Unlike site-to-site VPNs, a **Remote Access VPN** connects individual clients to a central gateway, creating secure tunnels so users can safely reach files, intranets, and applications from anywhere. Following is a step-by-step process to implement the remote access VPN:

Sample 'server.ovpn' Configuration

Following is the sample configuration you can code it in your **server.ovpn** file:

```
port 1194
proto udp
dev tun
ca ca.crt
cert server.crt
key server.key
dh dh.pem
server 10.8.0.0 255.255.255.0
ifconfig-pool-persist ipp.txt
keepalive 10 120
tls-auth ta.key 0
cipher AES-256-CBC
persist-key
persist-tun
status openvpn-status.log
verb 3
```

After this, open the Windows Firewall and allow UDP 1194 inbound. And then start the OpenVPN server as a Windows service.

Sample 'client.ovpn' Configuration

The given below is the sample **client.ovpn** configuration:

```
client
dev tun
proto udp
```

```
remote [SERVER_PUBLIC_IP] 1194
resolv-retry infinite
nobind
persist-key
persist-tun
ca ca.crt
cert user1.crt
key user1.key
tls-auth ta.key 1
cipher AES-256-CBC
verb 3
```

After this, launch the OpenVPN GUI as Administrator and connect using the profile. On successful connection, the client receives a virtual IP (such as 10.8.0.2), and all routed traffic is encrypted to the VPN server.

If authentication fails, double-check certificate files and paths. If you can connect but cannot reach internal resources, verify server-side routing or push routes in the server config (push "route 192.168.10.0 255.255.255.0").

Summary

So, in this chapter, you got to grips with the nuts and bolts and the nitty-gritty of Virtual Private Networks as the basis for secure communication in both business and personal contexts. You got to grips with how VPNs work in theory by creating encrypted tunnels across public networks to protect data and enable safe remote access. You explored the major protocols, PPTP, L2TP/IPsec, OpenVPN, WireGuard, and SSL/TLS, and saw how each fits different security and deployment needs. You've already got experience of installing OpenVPN on Windows, creating keys and certificates, and writing configuration files to enable site-to-site and remote access tunnels. And, finally, you also got pretty good at sorting out common problems, from firewall blocks to authentication failures, and you learned how to automate connection checks and client rollouts for a strong, easy-to-manage VPN setup.

Chapter 6: Wireless Networks

Chapter Overview

In this chapter, you're going to take a look at the world of wireless networking, checking out the technologies that connect devices without the need for physical cables. You'll start with the basics of wireless networks, learning how different protocols like Wi-Fi, Bluetooth, and Zigbee are designed for different performance, power, and coverage needs.

Then you'll get into the nitty-gritty of the IEEE 802.11 standards, tracing their evolution from the early days of 802.11b through to Wi-Fi 6 and its advanced features for high-density environments. You'll get to do some practical coding exercises where you can query available SSIDs, check signal quality, connect to networks programmatically, and even enumerate nearby Bluetooth devices straight from your C++ applications. You'll also get to grips with Zigbee, learning how to set up and communicate with IoT nodes via COM ports on Windows. We'll be focusing a lot on wireless security standards, showing how networks have evolved from the vulnerable WEP through WPA2 and into the advanced protections of WPA3.

By the time you reach the end of the chapter, you'll get a good understanding of how wireless technologies work and you'll also gain hands-on skills to automate, monitor and secure them in real-world applications.

Introduction to Wireless Networks

It's pretty much all around us, isn't it? When you open your laptop and connect to Wi-Fi at home, or when your phone automatically switches from mobile data to your office wireless, you're relying on one of the most transformative technologies in networking and wireless communication. You might have guessed it – wireless networks don't need cables! This is because they transmit information through electromagnetic waves, which means they can be used anywhere, are flexible, and can be made as large or small as you need them to be, which was not always possible with wired networks.

Wireless networking is a whole bunch of different technologies. It's a pretty comprehensive umbrella, covering things like Wi-Fi for fast local connections, Bluetooth for personal devices, Zigbee for low-power IoT ecosystems, 4G and 5G for global coverage, and newer mesh solutions that connect everything from smart homes to industrial sensors. All of these technologies have been designed with a specific purpose in mind, and they're all optimised for a particular balance of speed, range, energy efficiency, and reliability. It's really important for engineers, developers and admins to understand these differences.

Backbone of Wireless Networks

At the core, wireless networking works by modulating digital data onto radio waves or infrared signals. Transmitters and receivers exchange packets according to agreed protocols. These protocols dictate everything from **frequency band usage**, to **error correction**, to **encryption**

rules.

For example, Wi-Fi uses the IEEE 802.11 family of standards to manage how access points and devices share the 2.4 GHz and 5 GHz spectrum. Bluetooth operates in the same unlicensed band but with different signaling patterns designed for short-range, low-power connections. Zigbee also uses 2.4 GHz, but with mesh networking capabilities that allow hundreds of devices to relay data efficiently across wide areas with minimal power draw. Cellular networks, on the other hand, work with licensed frequencies, leveraging carrier infrastructure to provide wide-area coverage.

Different Wireless Networks In-use

1. **Wi-Fi (802.11 family)**

   Wi-Fi dominates local wireless networking. It powers homes, offices, and public spaces, offering high throughput, low latency, and ease of deployment. A Wi-Fi access point can serve dozens of clients simultaneously. The evolution from **802.11b** (11 Mbps) to **Wi-Fi 6 (802.11ax, up to 10 Gbps)** has made Wi-Fi a reliable backbone for both consumer and enterprise-grade networking.

2. **Bluetooth and BLE (Bluetooth Low Energy)**

   Bluetooth is designed for short-range personal networks, think wireless keyboards, headsets, and file transfers between phones. BLE, a variant introduced with Bluetooth 4.0, emphasizes extremely low power consumption, enabling devices like smartwatches, beacons, and IoT sensors to run for years on a coin cell battery.

3. **Zigbee and Thread**

   Zigbee is a mesh protocol ideal for IoT environments, letting small devices relay messages between each other, extending coverage without consuming much power. Thread, a newer competitor, uses IPv6 to provide similar capabilities but with stronger interoperability across smart devices.

4. **Cellular Wireless (4G, 5G)**

   Cellular networks provide global wireless coverage through carrier infrastructure. 4G revolutionized mobile broadband, while 5G now enables ultra-low latency and massive IoT connections, supporting smart cities, autonomous vehicles, and industrial automation.

Apart from this, there is **NFC (Near Field Communication)** which is extremely short-range (a few centimeters), commonly used for contactless payments. Then there is **LoRaWAN,** a Long-range, low-bandwidth protocol optimized for IoT sensors spanning kilometers. We also have **Wi-Fi HaLow (802.11ah)** and it is considered to be the emerging standard operating in sub-1 GHz frequencies, extending Wi-Fi range while reducing energy use.

Wireless Standards

The **IEEE 802.11** family defines the backbone of Wi-Fi networks. Over time, new amendments improved bandwidth, frequency utilization, and device density handling. A quick progression looks like this:

- **802.11b (1999):** 2.4 GHz, 11 Mbps.
- **802.11g (2003):** 2.4 GHz, 54 Mbps.
- **802.11n (2009, Wi-Fi 4):** 2.4/5 GHz, up to 600 Mbps, introduced MIMO.
- **802.11ac (2014, Wi-Fi 5):** 5 GHz only, gigabit throughput, MU-MIMO.
- **802.11ax (2019, Wi-Fi 6):** Multi-gigabit throughput, orthogonal frequency-division multiple access (OFDMA), better device density.
- **802.11be (Wi-Fi 7, upcoming):** Expected to deliver >30 Gbps speeds, ultra-low latency, and extended channel widths.

The choice of standard isn't just about speed, it's also about the environment. In a crowded apartment block, 5 GHz Wi-Fi 5 or Wi-Fi 6 provides less interference. In industrial IoT deployments, Wi-Fi HaLow may soon provide superior coverage with less energy drain.

Wireless Security Standards

The security in wireless networks is non-negotiable. Because data travels "through the air," attackers can capture it without physical access. The wireless standards are evolved to address the following:

- **WEP (Wired Equivalent Privacy):** The first attempt at wireless encryption. Weak and broken; not safe for any modern use.
- **WPA (Wi-Fi Protected Access):** Improved with TKIP but still insecure today.
- **WPA2:** Introduced AES-CCMP, becoming the standard for nearly 15 years. Still widely used but vulnerable to brute force if passwords are weak.
- **WPA3:** Current gold standard, introduces Simultaneous Authentication of Equals (SAE), stronger encryption, and better resistance against dictionary attacks.

In enterprise deployments, WPA2-Enterprise and WPA3-Enterprise integrate with RADIUS servers, requiring certificate-based authentication rather than shared passwords, dramatically improving security for organizations.

Sample Program: Listing Available Wi-Fi Networks

While wireless hardware drivers handle most low-level details, as a C++ developer, you can query and control wireless connections using **Windows APIs**. For example, the Windows Native Wi-Fi API (WlanAPI) allows you to scan networks, connect to SSIDs, and query signal strength.

Let us check out it through the following sample program in which we will try to capture or request the available wireless networks which are open to connect:

```
#include <windows.h>
```

```
#include <wlanapi.h>
#include <iostream>
#pragma comment(lib, "wlanapi.lib")
int main() {
    HANDLE hClient = NULL;
    DWORD dwMaxClient = 2;
    DWORD dwCurVersion = 0;
    DWORD dwResult = WlanOpenHandle(dwMaxClient, NULL,
&dwCurVersion, &hClient);
    if (dwResult != ERROR_SUCCESS) {
        std::cerr << "WlanOpenHandle failed" << std::endl;
        return 1;
    }
    PWLAN_INTERFACE_INFO_LIST pIfList = NULL;
    if (WlanEnumInterfaces(hClient, NULL, &pIfList) ==
ERROR_SUCCESS) {
        for (int i = 0; i < (int)pIfList->dwNumberOfItems;
i++) {
            PWLAN_INTERFACE_INFO pIfInfo =
(WLAN_INTERFACE_INFO *)&pIfList->InterfaceInfo[i];
            PWLAN_AVAILABLE_NETWORK_LIST pBssList = NULL;
            if (WlanGetAvailableNetworkList(hClient, &pIfInfo-
>InterfaceGuid,
                                            0, NULL,
&pBssList) == ERROR_SUCCESS) {
                for (int j = 0; j < (int)pBssList-
>dwNumberOfItems; j++) {
                    PWLAN_AVAILABLE_NETWORK pBssEntry =
&pBssList->Network[j];
                    std::wcout << L"SSID: " << pBssEntry-
>dot11Ssid.ucSSID << std::endl;
                }
```

```
                WlanFreeMemory(pBssList);
            }
        }
    }
    if (pIfList) WlanFreeMemory(pIfList);
    WlanCloseHandle(hClient, NULL);
    return 0;
}
```

This will list SSIDs visible to your wireless adapter, and with modifications, you can connect, disconnect, or monitor signal strength.

The wireless networks aren't just conveniences, they are now mission-critical infrastructure. From **home automation** to **enterprise mobility** and **industrial IoT**, the choice of technology, standard, and security implementation directly affects performance, reliability, and safety.

Programming Wireless Fidelity (WiFi)

When you think of wireless networking, WiFi is the first technology that comes to mind. It's the lifeline of modern connectivity, linking laptops, smartphones, and IoT devices to the internet. While its conceptual framework is familiar, access points, radio signals, encryption, the deeper layer is where things become interesting for you as a C++ programmer. WiFi is not only about connecting but also about **controlling, scanning, and monitoring** networks programmatically.

At its core, a WiFi network has three pieces:

- **Access Point (AP)** which acts as the central hub, broadcasting SSIDs and handling authentication.
- **Client Devices** that are equipped with wireless adapters that can join a network.
- **Infrastructure** that includes routers, switches, and the internet gateway that APs link into.

On Windows, the WiFi control can be done through the **WlanAPI** library (**`wlanapi.dll`**). This API provides access to wireless interfaces, letting you:

- Enumerate WiFi adapters.
- Scan available networks.
- Connect/disconnect from an SSID.
- Query current signal strength and security type.

Scanning WiFi Networks

Following is a sample scripting to scan the WiFi networks around your near proximity:

```
#include <windows.h>
#include <wlanapi.h>
#include <iostream>
#pragma comment(lib, "wlanapi.lib")
int main() {
    HANDLE hClient = NULL;
    DWORD dwVersion = 0;
    if (WlanOpenHandle(2, NULL, &dwVersion, &hClient) !=
ERROR_SUCCESS) {
        std::cerr << "Failed to open handle to WLAN API" <<
std::endl;
        return 1;
    }
    PWLAN_INTERFACE_INFO_LIST pIfList = NULL;
    if (WlanEnumInterfaces(hClient, NULL, &pIfList) ==
ERROR_SUCCESS) {
        for (int i = 0; i < (int)pIfList->dwNumberOfItems;
i++) {
            PWLAN_INTERFACE_INFO pIfInfo = &pIfList-
>InterfaceInfo[i];
            PWLAN_AVAILABLE_NETWORK_LIST pNetworkList = NULL;
            if (WlanGetAvailableNetworkList(hClient, &pIfInfo-
>InterfaceGuid,
                                             0, NULL,
&pNetworkList) == ERROR_SUCCESS) {
                for (int j = 0; j < (int)pNetworkList-
>dwNumberOfItems; j++) {
                    std::wcout << L"SSID: "
                               << (wchar_t*)pNetworkList-
>Network[j].dot11Ssid.ucSSID
                               << L" | Signal Strength: "
```

```
                              << pNetworkList-
>Network[j].wlanSignalQuality << L"%"
                              << std::endl;
                }
                WlanFreeMemory(pNetworkList);
            }
        }
    }
    if (pIfList) WlanFreeMemory(pIfList);
    WlanCloseHandle(hClient, NULL);
    return 0;
}
```

Run this as Administrator, and it will list the SSIDs around you along with signal quality. With minor changes, you can filter WPA3-enabled networks or prioritize strong signals.

Connecting to a WiFi Network

Now if we want to connect the desired WIFi network, we can simply programmatically initiate a connection by supplying an XML profile describing the SSID and its security settings.

Following is sample script to do this:

```
<WLANProfile
xmlns="http://www.microsoft.com/networking/WLAN/profile/v1">
    <name>MyWiFi</name>
    <SSIDConfig>
        <SSID>
            <name>MyWiFi</name>
        </SSID>
    </SSIDConfig>
    <connectionType>ESS</connectionType>
    <connectionMode>manual</connectionMode>
    <MSM>
        <security>
```

```
            <authEncryption>
                <authentication>WPA2PSK</authentication>
                <encryption>AES</encryption>
                <useOneX>false</useOneX>
            </authEncryption>
            <sharedKey>
                <keyType>passPhrase</keyType>
                <protected>false</protected>
                <keyMaterial>MyPassword123</keyMaterial>
            </sharedKey>
        </security>
    </MSM>
</WLANProfile>
```

After the above, you then save this profile XML and use **`WlanSetProfile`** in C++ to register it, then call **`WlanConnect`** with the SSID name. This will make our program capable of **joining WiFi networks dynamically**.

Programming Bluetooth

If WiFi connects you to the internet, Bluetooth connects you to your personal devices. Devices such as wireless mice, keyboards, headphones, wearables, and even IoT sensors rely on it. Unlike WiFi, Bluetooth is optimized for **low power and short-range communication**.

The bluetooth operates in the 2.4 GHz ISM band but uses frequency hopping (1,600 hops/sec) to avoid interference. There are two key modes which are very common today:

- The one is **classic bluetooth** for continuous data exchange (headphones, file transfers).
- And the other is **bluetooth low energy (BLE)** for periodic, low-power transmissions (IoT devices, smart tags).

Now, on our Windows, we can do the bluetooth programming through the **Windows.Devices.Bluetooth** API. The C++ can interact with this using Windows Runtime components.

Discovering Nearby Bluetooth Devices

Following is a sample program that will discover all the nearby bluetooth devices that are near in the proximity:

```
#include <windows.devices.bluetooth.h>
#include <windows.devices.enumeration.h>
#include <iostream>
using namespace winrt;
using namespace Windows::Devices::Bluetooth;
using namespace Windows::Devices::Enumeration;
int main() {
    init_apartment();
    auto selector = BluetoothDevice::GetDeviceSelector();
    auto devices =
DeviceInformation::FindAllAsync(selector).get();
    for (auto const& device : devices) {
        std::wcout << L"Name: " << device.Name().c_str()
                   << L" | ID: " << device.Id().c_str() <<
std::endl;
    }
    return 0;
}
```

After this, compile with **/ZW** (C++/CX) or link against C++/WinRT. This code enumerates Bluetooth devices that your adapter can discover.

Connecting to Device (Headset / BLE Sensor)

Once we have discovered all the working bluetooth networks or the devices that have bluetooth technology around our windows, we then connect to them through the following sample program:

```
auto device = BluetoothDevice::FromIdAsync(deviceId).get();
if (device) {
    std::wcout << L"Connected to device: " <<
device.Name().c_str() << std::endl;
}
```

After following the above program, we then get connected to the devices, and then we can query services like **RFCOMM (serial port emulation)** or BLE GATT profiles to exchange data with the device.

Programming Zigbee

Zigbee Overview

Coming to Zigbee, it is a low-power, low-data-rate wireless communication protocol built on IEEE 802.15.4. Unlike WiFi or Bluetooth, it's not designed for high-bandwidth streaming or fast internet browsing. Instead, Zigbee is optimized for **sensor networks**, **home automation**, and **industrial monitoring**, where devices only need to send small packets occasionally but must run for months or years on tiny batteries.

Following are some of the key features of Zigbee:

- Operates on **frequency bands,** primarily 2.4 GHz (global), with some use in 868 MHz (EU) and 915 MHz (US).
- The **range** is typically 10–100 meters, extended via mesh networking.
- Adopts **mesh topology** due to which the devices can act as **coordinators**, **routers**, or **end devices**.
- The **data rates** goes up to 250 kbps, sufficient for sensor readings, control messages, or small status updates.
- The **power efficiency** is simply amazing because of the sleep/wake cycles making Zigbee ideal for battery-operated IoT devices.

The applications of Zigbee includes smart lighting (Philips Hue), smart meters, industrial monitoring, healthcare, and agriculture sensors. Unlike WiFi, where you mainly connect to a single access point, Zigbee thrives in distributed systems where hundreds of devices talk to each other across a mesh.

Interacting with Zigbee Module

To work with Zigbee in practice, you typically use a **USB dongle or development kit** such as:

- Digi XBee USB adapters.
- TI CC2531 USB dongles.
- NXP or Silicon Labs Zigbee development kits.

These expose a serial interface (COM port in Windows) which you can control programmatically in C++. Following is a sample program that teaches us to talk to a zigbee module by means of a serial port:

```
#include <windows.h>

#include <iostream>

int main() {
```

```
    HANDLE hSerial = CreateFile(L"COM3",
                                GENERIC_READ | GENERIC_WRITE,
                                0, NULL, OPEN_EXISTING, 0,
NULL);
    if (hSerial == INVALID_HANDLE_VALUE) {
        std::cerr << "Error opening COM port" << std::endl;
        return 1;
    }
    DCB dcbSerialParams = {0};
    dcbSerialParams.DCBlength = sizeof(dcbSerialParams);
    if (!GetCommState(hSerial, &dcbSerialParams)) {
        std::cerr << "Error getting state" << std::endl;
        return 1;
    }
    dcbSerialParams.BaudRate = CBR_9600;
    dcbSerialParams.ByteSize = 8;
    dcbSerialParams.StopBits = ONESTOPBIT;
    dcbSerialParams.Parity   = NOPARITY;
    if (!SetCommState(hSerial, &dcbSerialParams)) {
        std::cerr << "Error setting state" << std::endl;
        return 1;
    }
    const char* cmd = "ATID 1234\r"; // Example: set PAN ID
    DWORD bytesWritten;
    WriteFile(hSerial, cmd, strlen(cmd), &bytesWritten, NULL);
    char buffer[256];
    DWORD bytesRead;
    ReadFile(hSerial, buffer, sizeof(buffer), &bytesRead,
NULL);
    buffer[bytesRead] = '\0';
```

```
    std::cout << "Response: " << buffer << std::endl;
    CloseHandle(hSerial);
    return 0;
}
```

The above program works like,

- It first opens a COM port connected to your Zigbee dongle.
- Then, it sends AT commands (e.g., **ATID** for PAN ID, **ATMY** for device address, **ATDL** for destination address).
- It then receive responses from the module.

After this, you can build simple programs to configure networks, send data frames, or monitor sensor readings. With libraries like **XBee C++ API**, you can very easily abstract this and directly send/receive Zigbee frames without manually parsing AT commands.

Wireless Standards 802.11a/b/g/n/ac/ax

When you move from Zigbee to WiFi standards, you're actually moving back to the IEEE 802.11 family. These are what made WiFi go from a weak 2 Mbps connection to super-fast multi-gigabit speeds.

The following list are the various wireless standards that were adopted worldwide:

1. **802.11a (1999)**
    - Frequency: 5 GHz
    - Speed: 54 Mbps
    - Early adoption was limited due to higher cost and shorter range compared to 2.4 GHz.
2. **802.11b (1999)**
    - Frequency: 2.4 GHz
    - Speed: 11 Mbps
    - Gained popularity due to cheaper equipment and better range.
3. **802.11g (2003)**
    - Frequency: 2.4 GHz
    - Speed: 54 Mbps
    - Backward-compatible with 802.11b.

4. **802.11n (2009, Wi-Fi 4)**
    - Dual-band (2.4 GHz and 5 GHz).
    - Speed: Up to 600 Mbps with MIMO (multiple antennas).
    - Revolutionized streaming and multimedia use.
5. **802.11ac (2014, Wi-Fi 5)**
    - Frequency: 5 GHz
    - Speed: Up to several Gbps.
    - Introduced MU-MIMO and beamforming, supporting high-density environments.
6. **802.11ax (2019, Wi-Fi 6)**
    - Frequency: 2.4 GHz and 5 GHz (and Wi-Fi 6E on 6 GHz).
    - Speed: 10+ Gbps, supports OFDMA and uplink MU-MIMO.
    - Designed for IoT and dense urban spaces.

Most of the modern WiFi adapters support multiple standards simultaneously. In our C++ learning journey, you cannot "force" the standard directly. The OS and driver will begin to negotiate based on both AP and client capabilities. But you can query the connected standard and ensure your code adapts.

Let us take the following sample program on querying the WiFi connection properties using the WlanAPI:

```
PWLAN_CONNECTION_ATTRIBUTES pConnectInfo = NULL;
DWORD connectInfoSize = sizeof(WLAN_CONNECTION_ATTRIBUTES);
WLAN_OPCODE_VALUE_TYPE opCode;
if (WlanQueryInterface(hClient, &pIfInfo->InterfaceGuid,
                       wlan_intf_opcode_current_connection,
                       NULL, &connectInfoSize,
                       (PVOID*)&pConnectInfo, &opCode) ==
ERROR_SUCCESS) {
    std::wcout << L"Connected SSID: " << pConnectInfo-
>wlanAssociationAttributes.dot11Ssid.ucSSID << std::endl;
    std::wcout << L"PHY Type: " << pConnectInfo-
>wlanAssociationAttributes.dot11PhyType << std::endl;
}
```

In the above, the **`dot11PhyType`** field reveals whether you're on 802.11n, ac, or ax. You can log this to monitor performance across devices.

In real word and that too in large enterprises, it is very widely enforcing the WPA3 on WiFi 6 APs.

Wireless Security Standards

The thing about wireless networking is that it's just more exposed than wired communication. There's no physical cable between the endpoints, so anyone within range can pick up the signals. This makes security standards essential. Eventually, the Wi-Fi Alliance and IEEE came up with a bunch of security measures that gradually fixed problems and made crypto more robust.

Popular Wireless Security Standards

Following are the various wireless security standards that are widely recognized and adopted in case-to-case baiss:

WEP (Wired Equivalent Privacy)

The first attempt at securing Wi-Fi was WEP, which was designed to offer "equivalent" protection to wired Ethernet. It used RC4 for encryption, with static keys (40-bit or 104-bit) combined with a 24-bit initialisation vector (IV). The design flaw was obvious: IVs were repeated quickly, making the system vulnerable to key recovery attacks. These days, everyone thinks WEP is totally broken and you should never use it.

WPA (Wi-Fi Protected Access)

As a patch to WEP, WPA introduced TKIP (Temporal Key Integrity Protocol), which dynamically generated keys per packet. This addressed some of WEP's flaws but retained RC4 under the hood, leaving WPA weaker against modern attacks. WPA is also deprecated and insecure today.

WPA2

WPA2 was pretty much the standard for over 10 years. The new version replaced RC4 with AES (Advanced Encryption Standard) in CCMP (Counter Mode Cipher Block Chaining Message Authentication Code Protocol). While WPA2-Personal uses pre-shared keys (PSK), WPA2-Enterprise relies on 802.1X with RADIUS servers, enabling per-user credentials. It's fair to say that WPA2 is still pretty popular, but there's still a big risk of dictionary attacks against weak PSKs.

WPA3

The current gold standard, WPA3 introduces Simultaneous Authentication of Equals (SAE), replacing the vulnerable PSK method. SAE provides forward secrecy, meaning even if a password is compromised later, past sessions remain secure. WPA3 also mandates 192-bit encryption in Enterprise mode and resists offline dictionary attacks.

Querying Security Standards

You can use the same WlanAPI as in earlier Wi-Fi examples to see what security standard your adapter is currently using.

```
PWLAN_AVAILABLE_NETWORK_LIST pBssList = NULL;

if (WlanGetAvailableNetworkList(hClient, &pIfInfo->InterfaceGuid,

                                0, NULL, &pBssList) == ERROR_SUCCESS) {

    for (int j = 0; j < (int)pBssList->dwNumberOfItems; j++) {

        PWLAN_AVAILABLE_NETWORK pBssEntry = &pBssList->Network[j];

        std::wcout << L"SSID: " << (wchar_t*)pBssEntry->dot11Ssid.ucSSID

                   << L" | Auth: " << pBssEntry->dot11DefaultAuthAlgorithm

                   << L" | Cipher: " << pBssEntry->dot11DefaultCipherAlgorithm

                   << std::endl;

    }

}
```

In the above, the **dot11DefaultAuthAlgorithm** and **dot11DefaultCipherAlgorithm** fields tell you whether the network uses WPA2, WPA3, or legacy WEP. In diagnostics tools, logging these values helps enforce policy, such as, for example, flagging insecure WEP/WPA networks.

If you can, make sure you use WPA3. For businesses, it's a good idea to combine WPA2/WPA3 with 802.1X and certificates. We need to keep an eye on and record client connections to stop downgrade attacks. When it comes to SSIDs, it's best to stick with "open" ones unless you're using them for guest networks. Even then, it's worth thinking about captive portals and VLAN isolation.

Summary

In this chapter, you took a look at the different wireless networking technologies that power both personal and industrial connectivity. You learned how Wi-Fi, Bluetooth, Zigbee and related standards form the backbone of wireless communication, each one optimised for different use cases. You got to grips with the technical details of the IEEE 802.11 standards, following the evolution from the early versions to Wi-Fi 6 and Wi-Fi 6E, and you learned how to use C++ to programmatically query and interact with these networks on Windows. You also understood the role of Zigbee in IoT, focusing on low-power, mesh-based communication and learning how to program devices through COM port interfaces.

You learned how to discover and connect to nearby devices using Bluetooth programming through Windows APIs. Wi-Fi programming went into more detail, teaching you how to scan SSIDs, connect with XML profiles, and check active PHY standards. Finally, we explored wireless security standards, looking at WEP, WPA, WPA2, and WPA3, and how to detect and enforce security in your applications. You've now got the know-how to manage, monitor and secure wireless environments programmatically, thanks to this hands-on, conceptual teaching.

Chapter 7: Asynchronous Programming

Chapter Overview

Think about a synchronous HTTP server that can only handle a few hundred client requests before performance starts to drop, with each request blocking the next one until it's finished. On the other hand, an asynchronous HTTP server can handle thousands of connections at once without any problems, because each request is sent to the system and control returns straight away to the event loop. In this chapter, you'll find out how asynchronous programming changes the way networking applications are designed, making them scalable, responsive, and efficient. First, you'll get to grips with the idea of asynchronous execution and why it's so important for systems that have to handle a lot of operations at the same time without getting stuck. Then you'll explore how callbacks, promises and async-style constructs bring non-blocking behaviour into your C++ code, and how each approach helps in different programming scenarios.

The chapter will also guide you through multithreading and concurrency, showing you how to spread workloads across CPU cores for true parallelism. You'll get to grips with asynchronous I/O and how event-driven programming works at the operating system level, with libraries like libuv making complex APIs easier to use. By the time you're done with this chapter, you'll get why asynchronous programming is so important and you'll have all the coding skills you need to make it work in C++ when building network applications that can handle real-world workloads.

Getting Started with Asynchronous Programming

When you think of networking programs, what makes them powerful isn't just that they can open sockets and send packets; it's how well they handle **many things happening at once**. Let us say that you are writing a file transfer service. A single client might be uploading a large file, another might be waiting for a download to finish, and yet another could be simply authenticating to the server. If your code handles these requests **one by one in sequence**, performance suffers immediately. A slow client holds everyone else hostage.

This is the exact problem that **asynchronous programming** solves. Instead of tying your program's flow to a single blocking operation, like waiting for data to arrive over a socket, you let the system carry on with other tasks. When the blocked operation eventually finishes, the system signals your code so you can handle the result. In other words, your program is no longer stalled by the slowest connection, the slowest disk read, or the slowest computation. It keeps moving, always responsive.

Now here, the networking applications can't afford that. The clients connect, disconnect, send data, or wait for responses constantly. A slow disk read, a network packet delayed by milliseconds, or a busy connection could freeze the entire system if handled synchronously. The asynchronous programming changes the model. Instead of blocking, it says, "Go ahead with other tasks while I wait, and I will let you know when this one is ready." That makes the restaurant model more like a busy kitchen with multiple cooks working in parallel and waiters calling out orders as soon as meals are done.

Concept of Asynchronous Programming

At its heart, asynchronous programming is about **non-blocking operations**. You start a task, say, sending a file over TCP, without waiting for it to finish. The operating system and networking stack handle the low-level work. When the transfer is complete, your code is notified through a callback, a future, or some other mechanism. This model allows a single-threaded program to juggle hundreds or even thousands of connections, keeping resources minimal and performance high. For networking, where waiting on external devices is common, this approach turns wasted time into usable processing cycles.

When it comes to networking, you can never be sure what's going to happen. A packet can arrive straight away or it might take a few seconds. A client might respond quickly, or get stuck in the middle of a transfer. If your program gets blocked during these waits, your CPU basically idles, and if you do this to lots of clients, your server will become unresponsive.

So with asynchronous programming:

- You can **accept new clients** while existing ones are still processing.
- You can **send and receive data in parallel** without creating hundreds of threads.
- You maintain **responsiveness**, which is critical in real-time systems like chat servers, online games, and streaming platforms.

Asynchronous in Real Systems

Now you must also be knowing that the C++ brings two unique advantages for asynchronous programming:

1. One is that you will have direct control over memory, threads, and system calls. This ensures low-latency operations and predictable performance under heavy loads.
2. And, the other is the access to various tools like **std::async**, **std::future**, and the industry-proven **Boost.Asio**, using these, the C++ developers can write asynchronous programs that scale across thousands of concurrent connections with relatively little overhead.

For example, the Boost.Asio uses asynchronous I/O with event loops, letting you run many socket operations simultaneously without spawning a new thread for each. This is precisely the kind of efficiency needed in networking.

Just think about how you'd go about building a basic HTTP server. In a synchronous model, it can handle one request at a time: it'll receive a client connection, process the request, send the response, and then move on. If you've got 1,000 clients using the system at the same time, it'll all go a bit weird.

An asynchronous server, on the other hand, can handle all 1,000 connections at once. While one request is waiting on a database, another can already send a response. The event loop only wakes up the right handler when the data is ready. That's why modern web servers, messaging brokers and IoT gateways are all built on asynchronous patterns.

Callbacks, Promises, and Async/Await

Callbacks

Callbacks are the simplest way to handle asynchronous results. You pass a function (or lambda) as a parameter, and that function gets invoked when the operation completes.

Let us take the following example on implementing the callback with Boost.Asio:

```
#include <boost/asio.hpp>
#include <iostream>
using boost::asio::ip::tcp;
void handleConnect(const boost::system::error_code& ec) {
    if (!ec) {
        std::cout << "Connected successfully!" << std::endl;
    } else {
        std::cout << "Connection failed: " << ec.message() <<
std::endl;
    }
}
int main() {
    boost::asio::io_context io;
    tcp::socket socket(io);
    tcp::resolver resolver(io);
    auto endpoints = resolver.resolve("gitforgits.com", "80");
    boost::asio::async_connect(socket, endpoints,
handleConnect);
    io.run();
    return 0;
}
```

Here, **handleConnect** is called only when the connection attempt finishes. The rest of your program can continue while the OS manages the actual network operation.

Promises and Futures

The callbacks can quickly become messy with deep nesting (callback hell). So here, the C++ provides **promises and futures** to make asynchronous code easier to reason about.

To understand better, you can follow the below sample program on using **std::promise/std::future**:

```
#include <future>
#include <thread>
#include <iostream>
void asyncTask(std::promise<int> prom) {
    std::this_thread::sleep_for(std::chrono::seconds(1));
    prom.set_value(42);
}
int main() {
    std::promise<int> prom;
    std::future<int> fut = prom.get_future();
    std::thread worker(asyncTask, std::move(prom));
    std::cout << "Waiting for result..." << std::endl;
    int value = fut.get();
    std::cout << "Got value: " << value << std::endl;
    worker.join();
}
```

This is synchronous at the call site (**fut.get()** blocks), but the heavy lifting is offloaded to another thread, showing how futures can coordinate results cleanly.

Async/Await

Unlike JavaScript or Python, C++ has no direct **async/await** syntax. Instead, you simulate it with **std::async**, which returns a **std::future**.

Let us understand through the following sample program of simulating using the **std::async**:

```
#include <future>
```

```
#include <iostream>

int calculate() {

    std::this_thread::sleep_for(std::chrono::seconds(2));

    return 100;

}

int main() {

    std::future<int> fut = std::async(std::launch::async,
calculate);

    std::cout << "Doing other work while calculating..." <<
std::endl;

    int result = fut.get(); // Blocks only when needed

    std::cout << "Calculation result: " << result <<
std::endl;

}
```

This gives you asynchronous execution with simple syntax, resembling **await** behavior in other languages.

So here altogether, you can build a toolkit of asynchronous programming patterns. Each one plays a role depending on the complexity of your application. The function of Networking, with its heavy reliance on I/O, benefits directly from these techniques, and thereby allows you to scale applications without wasting CPU cycles.

Writing Asynchronous using Callbacks

You've just seen why asynchronous programming is not an optional trick but a necessity in networking. Conceptually, it's clear that blocking operations waste CPU cycles and prevent scalability. The question becomes: **how do you actually write asynchronous code in C++?** The first answer lies in the most direct tool available, **callbacks.**

In the previous topic, we learned that the callback is simply a function you pass along with an operation. The system calls this function back once the operation is finished. In networking, this pattern is natural: you start sending or receiving data, and you provide a callback that is triggered when the data transfer completes. You may simply think of it like leaving your phone number with a shopkeeper. You don't stand at the counter until your order is ready, you go about your day, and the shopkeeper "calls you back" once the order is complete.

One better way to understand is to practically try to implement the asynchronous TCP Echo Client using the Callback. For this, we will write a simple client that connects to a server, sends a message, and waits for the response without blocking the main thread.

Following is the sample program:

```
#include <boost/asio.hpp>
#include <iostream>
using boost::asio::ip::tcp;
void onWrite(const boost::system::error_code& ec, std::size_t bytes) {
    if (!ec) {
        std::cout << "Message sent successfully (" << bytes << " bytes)." << std::endl;
    } else {
        std::cout << "Write failed: " << ec.message() << std::endl;
    }
}
void onRead(const boost::system::error_code& ec, std::size_t bytes, char* buffer) {
    if (!ec) {
        std::cout << "Server replied: " << std::string(buffer, bytes) << std::endl;
    } else {
        std::cout << "Read failed: " << ec.message() << std::endl;
    }
}
int main() {
    boost::asio::io_context io;
    tcp::resolver resolver(io);
    auto endpoints = resolver.resolve("127.0.0.1", "8080");
    tcp::socket socket(io);
    boost::asio::connect(socket, endpoints);
```

```
    std::string message = "Hello from client!";
    boost::asio::async_write(socket,
boost::asio::buffer(message),
                             onWrite);
    char buffer[128];
    socket.async_read_some(boost::asio::buffer(buffer, 128),
                           std::bind(onRead,
std::placeholders::_1,
                                     std::placeholders::_2,
buffer));
    io.run();
}
```

In the above,

- The client sends a message without blocking.
- The **onWrite** callback is invoked once the message leaves the socket.
- The **onRead** callback is triggered when data arrives from the server.
- Meanwhile, the main thread continues executing **io.run()**, which drives the event loop.

This above simple structure demonstrates why callbacks are so powerful in networking, they let your application remain responsive while background I/O completes.

Multithreading and Concurrency

In the previous topic, we saw how the callbacks solve a fundamental problem: they keep your application responsive by letting I/O complete in the background. However, callbacks alone don't take advantage of the multiple cores sitting inside modern CPUs. Imagine a server that must encrypt messages, log activity, or perform computations alongside socket I/O. If all of that runs on a single core, you're back to creating bottlenecks, just in a different place. This is where **multithreading and concurrency** step in. You don't abandon callbacks; you combine them with multiple threads, giving your program both responsiveness and raw parallel power.

When we talk about concurrency, it means your program can manage multiple tasks in overlapping timeframes, but not necessarily in parallel. For instance, a single core may switch rapidly between tasks. Similarly, the parallelism, on the other hand, means tasks literally run at the same time on different cores.

The networking function benefits from both, as the:

- **Concurrency** ensures multiple I/O operations are managed without waiting. And,
- **Parallelism** allows CPU-bound tasks (like encryption or compression) to run in true parallel threads.

Let us learn through a quick practical setup of implementing Multi-Threaded Asynchronous Server, by which we can scale a simple TCP server across multiple threads using Boost.Asio. Following is the sample program:

```
#include <boost/asio.hpp>
#include <thread>
#include <iostream>
#include <vector>
using boost::asio::ip::tcp;
void session(tcp::socket socket) {
    try {
        char data[1024];
        for (;;) {
            std::size_t length =
socket.read_some(boost::asio::buffer(data));
            boost::asio::write(socket,
boost::asio::buffer(data, length));
        }
    } catch (std::exception& e) {
        std::cerr << "Session error: " << e.what() <<
std::endl;
    }
}
int main() {
    try {
        boost::asio::io_context io;
        tcp::acceptor acceptor(io, tcp::endpoint(tcp::v4(),
8080));
        std::cout << "Server running on port 8080..." <<
std::endl;
```

```
        std::vector<std::thread> threads;
        // Launch multiple worker threads
        for (int i = 0; i <
std::thread::hardware_concurrency(); i++) {
            threads.emplace_back([&io]() { io.run(); });
        }
        for (;;) {
            tcp::socket socket(io);
            acceptor.accept(socket);
            std::thread(session, std::move(socket)).detach();
        }
        for (auto& t : threads) t.join();
    } catch (std::exception& e) {
        std::cerr << "Server error: " << e.what() <<
std::endl;
    }
}
```

From the above program, we can learn that the **`io_context`** can be serviced by multiple threads, spreading tasks across CPU cores. And, each new client runs in its own session thread, enabling true parallelism for socket handling.

Asynchronous I/O using 'libuv'

You've already seen how callbacks and concurrency make networking programs responsive. But the real magic comes when you combine these concepts with the **operating system's I/O facilities.** The Asynchronous I/O (also called as the AIO) means that instead of asking the OS to "read this socket" and blocking until data arrives, you issue a request and let the OS notify you when the operation is complete.

On Windows, this is implemented through mechanisms like **I/O Completion Ports (IOCP)**. On Linux, it's **`epoll`** or **`newer io_uring`**. However, managing these details manually can get complicated, which is why libraries exist to abstract it away. One of the most widely used is **libuv.**

What is libuv?

The Libuv is a cross-platform asynchronous I/O library originally developed for Node.js but used far beyond that ecosystem today. It provides:

- An event loop that works consistently across platforms.
- Non-blocking filesystem, socket, and timer operations.
- Thread pool support for CPU-bound tasks.
- A simple, callback-driven API.

What makes libuv special for you as a C++ developer is that it gives you direct access to asynchronous networking and filesystem operations **without tying you to Node.js or any higher-level runtime.** It runs on Windows, Linux, and macOS with the same API. Also, the libuv saves you from manually dealing with IOCP while still giving you its performance benefits. In the following, we will take you through building a basic **TCP echo server** using libuv, in which we will demonstrate you the event loop in action, and thereby handling the multiple clients asynchronously.

Installing 'Libuv'

To begin with, we get the libuv installed, which is available via https://libuv.org. And, then we link it into our C++ project.

```
#include <uv.h>

#include <iostream>

#include <cstring>
```

Define Callback for Reading Data

In the above, we then define the callback so as to facilitate the reading of the incoming data from the client:

```
void allocBuffer(uv_handle_t* handle, size_t suggested_size,
uv_buf_t* buf) {

    buf->base = (char*)malloc(suggested_size);

    buf->len = suggested_size;

}

void echoRead(uv_stream_t* client, ssize_t nread, const
uv_buf_t* buf) {

    if (nread > 0) {

        uv_write_t* req =
(uv_write_t*)malloc(sizeof(uv_write_t));

        uv_buf_t wrbuf = uv_buf_init(buf->base, nread);
```

```
        uv_write(req, client, &wrbuf, 1, [](uv_write_t* req,
int status) {
            if (status) std::cerr << "Write error: " <<
uv_strerror(status) << std::endl;
            free(req);
        });
        return;
    }
    if (nread < 0) {
        if (nread != UV_EOF)
            std::cerr << "Read error: " << uv_err_name(nread)
<< std::endl;
        uv_close((uv_handle_t*)client, NULL);
    }
    free(buf->base);
}
```

This callback echoes the data back using **uv_write**. If the client disconnects, it closes the handle.

Handle New Connections

We now then program a callback which will trigger if any new client connects.

```
void onNewConnection(uv_stream_t* server, int status) {
    if (status < 0) {
        std::cerr << "New connection error: " <<
uv_strerror(status) << std::endl;
        return;
    }
    uv_tcp_t* client = (uv_tcp_t*)malloc(sizeof(uv_tcp_t));
    uv_tcp_init(server->loop, client);
    if (uv_accept(server, (uv_stream_t*)client) == 0) {
        uv_read_start((uv_stream_t*)client, allocBuffer,
echoRead);
```

```
    } else {
        uv_close((uv_handle_t*)client, NULL);
    }
}
```

This callback accepts the connection and starts reading asynchronously.

Create Server

After this, we then finally create the server:

```
int main() {
    uv_loop_t* loop = uv_default_loop();
    uv_tcp_t server;
    uv_tcp_init(loop, &server);
    sockaddr_in addr;
    uv_ip4_addr("0.0.0.0", 8080, &addr);
    uv_tcp_bind(&server, (const struct sockaddr*)&addr, 0);
    int r = uv_listen((uv_stream_t*)&server, 128,
onNewConnection);
    if (r) {
        std::cerr << "Listen error: " << uv_strerror(r) <<
std::endl;
        return 1;
    }
    std::cout << "Echo server running on port 8080..." <<
std::endl;
    uv_run(loop, UV_RUN_DEFAULT);
    return 0;
}
```

From the above program, the **uv_run()** function drives the application and handles events. The **uv_read_start** is ready to listen for data, but it won't block anything. In addition, the **EchoRead** is only triggered when data arrives.

Also, the server can handle a bunch of clients with just one thread, and all thanks goes to the **libuv's** super efficient event loop. So, with this design, your server doesn't waste time waiting for any single client. Every connection is managed asynchronously, and the event loop makes sure callbacks are dispatched promptly. This is the same model used by massive systems like Node.js web servers, but here you're writing it directly in C++ with full control.

Summary

So, in this chapter you learnt everything there was to know about asynchronous programming and how it works in networking applications! You found out that asynchronous programming got rid of the bottlenecks of synchronous blocking operations, meaning it could handle thousands of concurrent connections efficiently. You looked at how callbacks were the base of asynchronous code, meaning your programs could react when I/O events were finished without blocking the main flow. Then you saw how concurrency and multithreading took this idea even further by spreading workloads across CPU cores, making sure you were always responsive even when there was a lot going on.

The chapter took you deeper into asynchronous I/O, where the operating system itself tells your program about completed operations, and you studied how libraries such as libuv make working with event loops and non-blocking sockets on Windows easier. Overall, you've got a step-by-step walkthrough to writing clients and servers that use callbacks, promises, and asynchronous event loops, so you've got both the ideas and the hands-on coding experience.

Chapter 8: Network Testing and Simulation

Chapter Overview

This chapter's gonna teach you how pros validate and evaluate networks using structured testing methodologies and powerful simulation environments. First, you'll get to grips with the different types of network testing, such as functional testing, which checks that components behave as expected, and performance testing, which measures throughput, latency, and jitter under realistic loads. Then you'll learn how stress testing shows how the system behaves under extreme or unusual conditions, and how security testing makes sure the defences are up to scratch against custom attacks or malformed packets. Each of these methods will be shown not only in theory but in practice too, using C++ programs that craft packets, generate traffic and measure results, so that you get hands-on experience as well as theoretical understanding.

Once you're feeling confident with physical testing, the chapter will show you how to use network simulation to model complex topologies and scenarios without having to use physical hardware. You'll get to try out different simulators and then focus on NS-3, the tool of choice for research, which lets you build, configure and analyse virtual networks with a high level of realism. By the time you're done with this chapter, you're going to have a dual skill set: the ability to test live networks programmatically and to explore hypothetical designs through simulation.

Network Testing Methodologies

When you first set up a network, it's tempting to feel satisfied once the basic connectivity checks succeed. You ping a host, receive replies, maybe open a web page, and assume the network is good. But as soon as users begin relying on that network for real workloads, streaming video, transferring files, authenticating securely, hidden problems start to surface. Perhaps latency spikes under load, or a firewall rule fails to block a specific packet type. This is why seasoned professionals never rely on surface-level checks. Instead, they apply **structured testing methodologies** that allow them to validate the network from multiple angles.

You can think of it like a medical examination in which a quick look may tell you a patient is breathing, but only a structured examination, measuring heart rate, blood pressure, reflexes, and performing scans, gives the full picture of health. The networks demand the same rigor. The different methodologies target different layers of reliability, performance, and security, so that when combined, they provide confidence that the system is production-ready.

Functional Testing

The first step is always to ask: does the network do what it was designed to do? This is the essence of functional testing. If a router should forward packets from subnet A to subnet B, does it? If a firewall should block traffic from a banned IP, does it consistently enforce the rule? Without confirming functional correctness, no other testing is meaningful. You wouldn't measure the speed of a car with a broken engine; you confirm it runs first.

Performance Testing

Once basic functions are validated, attention shifts to performance. This answers the question: can the network deliver expected service quality under normal workloads? Performance testing measures throughput, latency, jitter, and packet loss. For example, a video conferencing service may need latency below 50 ms and minimal jitter to remain usable. If the network introduces delay or packet reordering, the service becomes choppy. The performance testing highlights whether the infrastructure is suitable for real-world application requirements.

Stress Testing

Performance testing shows how the network behaves under expected conditions, but what about the unexpected? Stress testing deliberately pushes the network beyond its design limits. This might mean simulating thousands of simultaneous logins, flooding a link with near-saturation traffic, or generating protocol-level edge cases. The aim isn't to prove the network can survive anything, it's to reveal the breaking point and observe whether the system fails gracefully or catastrophically. A well-designed network may degrade under stress but should remain responsive and recover quickly.

Security Testing

Even a network that is functionally correct and high-performing is worthless if it's vulnerable to attack. Security testing probes defenses by simulating malicious behavior. Crafted packets test whether firewalls and intrusion detection systems respond correctly. The authentication processes are checked for weak credentials. Encrypted sessions are validated against downgrade attacks. The security testing is not just about preventing breaches; it's about ensuring that legitimate functionality does not expose unintended risks.

Modern environments are rarely homogeneous. You might have routers from one vendor, switches from another, and client devices running different operating systems. Compatibility testing verifies that these components interact seamlessly. For instance, if one router interprets TCP options differently from another, sessions may fail in subtle ways. The interoperability testing identifies these mismatches early, before users encounter unexplained failures. Each methodology provides unique insights, but together they create a layered safety net. The functional testing ensures correctness, performance testing validates service quality, stress testing exposes resilience, security testing verifies defenses, and compatibility testing ensures interoperability. Without them, the administrators are left reacting to failures in production instead of preventing them in advance. With them, you gain confidence that the network will deliver not only today but under future workloads and evolving threats. And because we are working with C++, you will see how these methodologies can be made repeatable and automated. By writing programs that simulate client sessions, generate traffic, and validate responses, you can perform these tests consistently, instead of relying only on manual observation. This is where functional testing, our next focus, comes alive.

Functional Testing

Now that you get where functional testing fits in, let's take a closer look. Basically, functional testing just checks that the networking gear is actually doing what it's meant to.

So, let's say you've got a firewall set up to block traffic from a restricted IP address. On paper, the configuration looks fine. But unless you send a packet from that IP and see if it's dropped, you can't be sure. And functional testing checks these behaviours directly. It doesn't measure speed or scalability; it just checks that the function is correct.

Scope of Functional Testing

The functional testing touches multiple aspects, including:

- **Connectivity** – can two endpoints establish sessions successfully?
- **Packet forwarding** – are packets routed correctly according to the routing table?
- **Protocol compliance** – does the system respect expected sequences like the TCP three-way handshake?
- **Access control** – do firewalls and ACLs enforce their policies without exceptions?
- **Configuration accuracy** – when changes are made (such as NAT rules or VLAN assignments), do they produce the expected effect?

Now here, if any of these functions are broken, performance or stress testing later becomes meaningless. That's why functional testing always comes first.

Functional Testing Procedure

The procedure is structured yet simple. First, you identify the specific function under test, for example, verifying that a router forwards packets from one subnet to another. Then, you prepare controlled test input, such as crafted packets representing traffic from subnet A destined for subnet B. You define the expected output: the packet should emerge at subnet B. Next, you execute the test by sending the traffic and observing the behavior. Finally, you compare the observed results to the expected ones. If they match, the function passes; if not, you review the configuration or suspect a fault. This procedure scales from simple pings to complex multi-protocol scenarios.

And, this is where C++ becomes powerful. Unlike black-box tools, C++ allows you to craft packets exactly as you want and inspect responses at the byte level. Libraries such as **PcapPlusPlus** or **libtins** give you programmatic control over packet construction and parsing. This allows you to automate tests that would otherwise require manual command-line utilities. For example, you can build packets that mimic specific TCP states, or create malformed DNS queries to see if the server responds correctly.

Sample Program: ICMP Echo Request

We'll use a sample program to show how to do functional testing, so you can check that a host processes ICMP echo requests (pings) correctly. You can use **PcapPlusPlus** to make an Ethernet + IPv4 + ICMP echo request packet, send it, and check the response.

Following is the sample script:

```
#include "Packet.h"
#include "IPv4Layer.h"
#include "IcmpLayer.h"
#include "EthLayer.h"
#include <iostream>
bool testICMPPacket() {
    pcpp::EthLayer
ethLayer(pcpp::MacAddress("11:22:33:44:55:66"),

pcpp::MacAddress("66:55:44:33:22:11"),
                            PCPP_ETHERTYPE_IP);
    pcpp::IPv4Layer ipLayer(pcpp::IPv4Address("192.168.1.10"),
                            pcpp::IPv4Address("192.168.1.1"));
    pcpp::IcmpLayer icmpLayer;
    icmpLayer.setEchoRequestData(1234, 1);
    pcpp::Packet packet(100);
    packet.addLayer(&ethLayer);
    packet.addLayer(&ipLayer);
    packet.addLayer(&icmpLayer);
    packet.computeCalculateFields();
    uint16_t expectedLen = ipLayer.getHeaderLen() +
icmpLayer.getHeaderLen();
    uint16_t actualLen = packet.getRawPacket()-
>getRawDataLen();
    return (actualLen >= expectedLen);
}
```

```
int main() {
    if (testICMPPacket())
        std::cout << "Functional test passed!" << std::endl;
    else
        std::cout << "Functional test failed!" << std::endl;
    return 0;
}
```

Now, when you run the above script, the program assembles an ICMP echo packet and checks that it meets expectations. It's although a minimal one but it is a clear example of functional testing. The function is "build a valid ICMP echo packet," and the expected outcome is "a correctly structured packet," and the program validates the result. For more exploration, you could craft a TCP SYN packet destined for a restricted port and send it through a firewall. The expected result is that the firewall drops it. If you receive a SYN-ACK in response, the firewall is misconfigured. The test would immediately reveal this.

To summarize, the functional testing is not glamorous, it doesn't show off throughput numbers or simulate massive loads. But it is foundational. The performance, stress, and security testing only matter if the basics are correct, and this is where the functional testing ensures that before you push the network to its limits, you know it is functionally sound.

Performance Testing

Now form the previous topic, once the functional testing confirms that the network behaves correctly, we then look into the next question, which is: **how well does it perform under realistic load?** A router may forward packets, and a firewall may enforce rules, but if throughput collapses under modest traffic or latency spikes make video calls unusable, then the network still fails in its mission. The performance testing addresses this by measuring the service quality of the network under expected operating conditions.

I'll give you an example. Let's say you're testing a new office network. We've run some basic tests, and it looks like DNS resolution is working, the routers are forwarding packets, and the firewalls are blocking unauthorized access. At this point, the basics look good. But when 200 employees start video meetings at the same time, things can go south fast. Video calls get interrupted, file transfers get slow, and the firewall's CPU usage goes through the roof. If we didn't do performance testing, these problems would only show up in production.

Performance Testing Evaluation

The performance testing focuses on several measurable indicators, including the:

- **Throughput**, which is the maximum rate at which data passes through the network.
- **Latency**, which is nothing but the time it takes for a packet to travel from source to destination.
- **Jitter**, is basically the variation in latency, which is especially harmful to real-time applications. And,
- **Packet loss**, which is the percentage of packets dropped under load.

Once you quantify all the above, you get a profile of how the network performs in realistic conditions.

Performance Testing Procedure

The testing procedure with regards to the performance typically follows a repeatable pattern. First, you define your performance targets, such as 1 Gbps throughput, latency below 50 ms, and jitter under 20 ms. Then, you prepare synthetic or real traffic loads that reflect actual usage, like multiple parallel file transfers or simulated video streams. Next, you execute these tests while monitoring the key metrics. Finally, you analyze whether the observed performance meets your targets. If it doesn't, you identify bottlenecks and tune configurations or hardware.

And in this regard too, the C++ is well-suited to performance testing because it allows you to generate and measure traffic with high precision. Our already learned library **Boost.Asio** provides strong control over sockets, while the **PcapPlusPlus** or **libtins** does let us craft raw packets. So, if we write our own test programs, we can replicate the realistic scenarios without relying solely on third-party tools.

Sample Program: TCP Throughput Measurement

We will implement a simple throughput test using Boost.Asio. So here, we will create a client that repeatedly sends data and a server that receives and measures the total bytes over time.

Following is the server script:

```
#include <boost/asio.hpp>

#include <iostream>

#include <chrono>

using boost::asio::ip::tcp;

int main() {

    boost::asio::io_context io;

    tcp::acceptor acceptor(io, tcp::endpoint(tcp::v4(),
8080));
```

```
    tcp::socket socket(io);
    acceptor.accept(socket);
    char buffer[8192];
    std::size_t totalBytes = 0;
    auto start = std::chrono::steady_clock::now();
    for (;;) {
        std::size_t bytesRead =
socket.read_some(boost::asio::buffer(buffer));
        totalBytes += bytesRead;
        auto elapsed =
std::chrono::duration_cast<std::chrono::seconds>(
            std::chrono::steady_clock::now() - start
        ).count();
        if (elapsed > 0) {
            double throughput = (totalBytes * 8.0) / (elapsed
* 1e6);
            std::cout << "Throughput: " << throughput << "
Mbps\r" << std::flush;
        }
    }
}
```

And, this is the client script:

```
#include <boost/asio.hpp>
#include <iostream>
#include <string>
using boost::asio::ip::tcp;
int main() {
    boost::asio::io_context io;
    tcp::resolver resolver(io);
    auto endpoints = resolver.resolve("127.0.0.1", "8080");
    tcp::socket socket(io);
```

```
    boost::asio::connect(socket, endpoints);
    std::string data(8192, 'X'); // 8KB payload
    for (;;) {
        boost::asio::write(socket, boost::asio::buffer(data));
    }
}
```

From the above scripts, the client continuously sends data to saturate the link. And, the server measures total bytes received and reports throughput over time. So, if you run this in a controlled environment, you can measure whether the network delivers the expected bandwidth. In addition, you can extend this to measure latency by timestamping packets or jitter by analyzing the variation in arrival times.

To me, the performance testing reveals whether the network meets real-world service requirements such as, if throughput looks fine for bulk transfers but latency spikes unpredictably, you know that VoIP or video conferencing will suffer.

Stress Testing

Stress Testing Purpose

In the previous, we have seen how the performance testing validates the behavior of the nertwork under expected loads. **But what happens when the unexpected occurs?** The users may suddenly surge, or a misconfiguration might generate a traffic storm. This is where stress testing is needed. The stress testing deliberately pushes the network beyond its design limits to reveal how it behaves under extreme conditions. You can think of stress testing like a crash test for vehicles. The cars aren't expected to hit walls at 80 km/h, but by testing them that way, engineers learn how they respond to catastrophic events. The networks are similar. The stress testing may never reflect normal conditions, but it reveals the network's resilience.

The purpose of stress testing isn't to achieve benchmarks, it's to expose weaknesses. Under stress, routers may exhaust their memory, firewalls may fail to apply rules, or applications may crash. A well-designed network should degrade gracefully: throughput may drop, latency may rise, but the system should remain responsive and recover when load decreases. If stress testing causes total collapse, redesign is required.

Stress Testing Procedure

The procedure starts by defining what kind of stress you want to apply. It might be **volume stress**, where you flood the network with packets, or **connection stress**, where you simulate thousands of simultaneous clients. Then, you prepare tools or programs that can generate such stress. You run the test while monitoring critical metrics like CPU usage, memory consumption, and packet drops. Finally, you evaluate how the system behaves: does it fail gracefully, or does it collapse entirely?

Once more, C++ is perfect for stress testing because it can handle a lot of traffic quickly. With raw sockets or libraries like Boost.Asio, you can simulate thousands of parallel connections. This lets you push the network to its limits in a controlled, repeatable way.

Sample Program: Simulating Connection Flood

Following is a simple program that creates multiple TCP connections to a server, simulating a surge of clients.

```
#include <boost/asio.hpp>
#include <iostream>
#include <vector>
#include <memory>
using boost::asio::ip::tcp;
int main() {
    boost::asio::io_context io;
    tcp::resolver resolver(io);
    auto endpoints = resolver.resolve("127.0.0.1", "8080");
    std::vector<std::shared_ptr<tcp::socket>> sockets;
    try {
        for (int i = 0; i < 1000; i++) {
            auto socket = std::make_shared<tcp::socket>(io);
            boost::asio::connect(*socket, endpoints);
            sockets.push_back(socket);
            std::cout << "Connection " << i + 1 << "
established." << std::endl;
        }
    } catch (std::exception& e) {
        std::cerr << "Error creating connections: " <<
e.what() << std::endl;
    }
```

```
    io.run();
}
```

From the above program, we let us understand how the stress testing takes place. The above program tries to establish 1000 simultaneous TCP connections. This actually stresses the server's connection-handling capacity. You can observe when the server starts refusing connections or when latency spikes. In addition, you can extend this further by sending random payloads through each connection, or by combining connection stress with throughput stress.

If you use the efficiency of C++ scripts to its best, you can easily create stress levels that quickly expose bottlenecks, such as socket exhaustion or memory leaks.

Security Testing

Core Benefit of Security Testing

A network may be functionally correct, perform well, and even hold up under stress, but it is still incomplete if its defenses are weak. Security testing ensures that the network cannot be bypassed, misused, or compromised by malicious traffic. Without security validation, even the most carefully designed systems are vulnerable.

One way of thinking it is like locking the doors of your home in which you may check that the windows open smoothly, the roof doesn't leak, and the heating system runs efficiently. But if the locks on the doors are flimsy, none of the other feature's matter, your home is unsafe. The security testing provides the assurance that the locks, alarms, and defenses of your network are reliable.

The security testing typically checks:

- **Access control**: Can unauthorized users gain entry?
- **Authentication**: Are passwords and certificates enforced properly?
- **Encryption**: Are sensitive communications protected against interception or downgrade?
- **Protocol robustness**: Do devices handle malformed packets gracefully without crashing?
- **Intrusion response**: Are attacks detected and logged by monitoring systems?

Unlike functional or performance testing, the emphasis of security testing is not on normal operations but rather on hostile and the abnormal conditions.

Security Testing Procedure

The process begins by identifying potential attack vectors. For example, a firewall may be tested for weak rules, a web server for unencrypted traffic, or a router for malformed packet handling. Next, test inputs are prepared, these may be crafted packets, replayed attack signatures, or brute-force connection attempts. The outputs are then observed: do the defenses hold, or do packets slip through? Finally, logs and alerts are examined to ensure the attack was not only blocked but also detected.

Here too, the C++ gives you fine-grained control over packet creation, making it possible to craft traffic that mimics real attacks. The **libtins** and the **PcapPlusPlus** let you modify fields, inject malformed headers, or replay traffic with slight alterations.

Sample Program: Malformed TCP Packet Injection

Let us try out the following program in which we construct a TCP packet with both SYN and FIN flags:

```
#include <tins/tins.h>
#include <iostream>
using namespace Tins;
int main() {
    NetworkInterface iface("Ethernet"); // Replace with your
interface
    PacketSender sender;
    // Create a TCP SYN packet with malformed flags
    EthernetII eth = EthernetII() /
                     IP("192.168.1.1", "192.168.1.100") /
                     TCP(80, 12345);
    TCP& tcp = eth.rfind_pdu<TCP>();
    tcp.set_flag(TCP::SYN, true);
    tcp.set_flag(TCP::FIN, true); // Illegal combination
    sender.send(eth, iface);
    std::cout << "Malformed TCP packet sent!" << std::endl;
}
```

In the above program, a TCP packet with both SYN and FIN flags set is established which should never occur in valid traffic. A correctly configured firewall should drop this packet, while a poorly configured or unpatched device might crash.

So, if you colufd understand properly, the security testing is not about generating every possible attack but about verifying that your defenses are active and effective. Here, you can directly test whether access control lists, intrusion detection systems, and firewall rules behave as intended. Without this testing, you are trusting security by assumption, which is never safe.

Network Simulations and NS-3

There are pros and cons to testing a live network. It's like trying to figure out how a new routing protocol will perform with thousands of nodes or how latency changes across a satellite link. Setting this up physically is expensive and time-consuming. It's a network simulation that offers a solution. All you have to do is create a virtual environment where traffic, devices, and topologies are modeled in software. It lets you try out different scenarios without any risk. You can test how a protocol behaves under different delays, how routing converges after a failure, or how QoS policies impact application performance.

Popular Network Simulators

There are several tools exist for this purpose, including:

- **ns-2** which is an older but once widely used simulator.
- **OMNeT++**, very popularly known for its modularity and graphical environment.
- **GNS3** being a graphical network emulator often used for Cisco labs.
- **Mininet** is specifically designed for software-defined networking (SDN) scenarios.
- **NS-3** is a modern, open-source discrete-event simulator with wide adoption.

Among these, the **NS-3** stands out for its realism, flexibility, and active support from researchers and professionals alike. The NS-3 models network stacks and protocols with significant fidelity. It supports IP, TCP, UDP, Wi-Fi, LTE, and more. You can build complex topologies, inject custom applications, and trace performance metrics in detail. It is written in C++ with Python bindings, making it a perfect fit for our journey.

Exploring NS-3

Fundamentally, NS-3 is a discrete-event simulator. This means time advances in steps according to events, like a packet being sent or a node receiving data. You can process each event in sequence, simulating networks over minutes or hours in just a few seconds of real time.

When you describe your network in code, you're talking about things like how many nodes there are, what protocols they use, and what kind of traffic flows between them After that, NS-3 simulates the behavior, and you can collect statistics like throughput, delay, and packet loss. This makes NS-3 a must for testing designs before rolling them out.

Installing NS-3

The best way to install NS-3 is through **Windows Subsystem for Linux (WSL)**, which allows Linux binaries to run seamlessly on Windows.

- Open PowerShell as Administrator and run:

```
wsl --install -d Ubuntu
```

- Update Packages in WSL

```
sudo apt update
sudo apt upgrade -y
```

- Install Dependencies

```
sudo apt install g++ python3 cmake ninja-build git -y
```

- Download NS-3

```
git clone https://gitlab.com/nsnam/ns-3-dev.git ns-3
cd ns-3
```

- Build NS-3

```
./ns3 configure --enable-examples --enable-tests
./ns3 build
```

Once built, you can run example simulations from the **examples/** directory.

Sample Program: Running Simulation in NS-3

Following is a simple simulation using NS-3 in which we will create two nodes connected by a point-to-point link and then sending the packets between them.

```
#include "ns3/core-module.h"
#include "ns3/network-module.h"
#include "ns3/internet-module.h"
#include "ns3/point-to-point-module.h"
#include "ns3/applications-module.h"
using namespace ns3;
int main() {
    NodeContainer nodes;
    nodes.Create(2);
    PointToPointHelper pointToPoint;
    pointToPoint.SetDeviceAttribute("DataRate",
StringValue("5Mbps"));
    pointToPoint.SetChannelAttribute("Delay",
StringValue("2ms"));
    NetDeviceContainer devices;
```

```
    devices = pointToPoint.Install(nodes);
    InternetStackHelper stack;
    stack.Install(nodes);
    Ipv4AddressHelper address;
    address.SetBase("10.1.1.0", "255.255.255.0");
    Ipv4InterfaceContainer interfaces =
address.Assign(devices);
    UdpEchoServerHelper echoServer(9);
    ApplicationContainer serverApps =
echoServer.Install(nodes.Get(1));
    serverApps.Start(Seconds(1.0));
    serverApps.Stop(Seconds(10.0));
    UdpEchoClientHelper echoClient(interfaces.GetAddress(1),
9);
    echoClient.SetAttribute("MaxPackets", UintegerValue(5));
    echoClient.SetAttribute("Interval",
TimeValue(Seconds(1.0)));
    echoClient.SetAttribute("PacketSize",
UintegerValue(1024));
    ApplicationContainer clientApps =
echoClient.Install(nodes.Get(0));
    clientApps.Start(Seconds(2.0));
    clientApps.Stop(Seconds(10.0));
    Simulator::Run();
    Simulator::Destroy();
    return 0;
}
```

When you execute it, the NS-3 simulates the traffic flow and logs packet exchanges, delays, and performance statistics. The physical testing tells you how your deployed network behaves, while this above simulation lets you experiment with topologies and protocols you haven't yet built. The NS-3 gets you to explore scenarios ranging from small LANs to large-scale wireless and mobile networks, all from your Windows machine via WSL.

Summary

To sum it up, you now know how network testing and simulation make sure a network works right, handles traffic, and stays safe against attacks. You know how testing methodologies form the foundation of validation . Then you moved on to performance testing, where you measured things like throughput, latency, jitter, and packet loss using C++ programs that generated and received traffic. That way, you could see if the networks were meeting the expected service levels.

The security testing taught us to craft packets and to make use of abnormal traffic flow to test firewalls, intrusion detection systems, and protocol resilience. Then you moved into the field of network simulation. There, you used computer models to create complex topologies instead of doing physical testing. We talked a bit about NS-3, and we went through the installation process on Windows using WSL. We also configured it, and I gave a demo to show how point-to-point traffic flows through the system. Overall, you got the skills to test real deployments and explore networks with the help of the NS-3 simulations.

Chapter 9: Network Configuration Management

Chapter Overview

In this chapter, you will learn how the management of configurations defines the stability, performance, and security of modern networks. You will begin by exploring the idea of configuration as the hidden blueprint behind every device, determining how packets are forwarded, which services are exposed, and how policies are enforced. From there, you will be introduced to NETCONF, the standardized protocol for programmatic configuration, and see how it allows you to retrieve and apply settings using structured RPCs instead of fragile CLI commands.

Next, you will then dive into everyday tasks, such as tuning TCP and UDP sockets for performance, running diagnostic tools automatically, and applying ACLs and firewall rules across multiple devices. You will also discover how to handle higher-risk activities like firmware updates with automation that reduces downtime, and how to build recovery strategies that bring devices back online when configurations or updates fail. By the time you complete this chapter, you will understand how to transform configuration management from a manual, error-prone process into a reliable, automated practice that protects networks against both mistakes and malicious threats.

Network Configurations Overview

When you think about a network, you usually think about the things you can see first: switches, routers, firewalls, and the cables or wireless links that connect them. However, the configuration applied to those devices is what truly defines how the network behaves, not just the hardware. The configuration is the invisible blueprint that determines how packets are forwarded, which traffic is allowed or blocked, which services are prioritized, and how securely communication takes place. Without proper configuration, even the most advanced hardware is little more than idle circuitry.

This chapter will teach you about the discipline of Network Configuration Management (NCM). In its most basic sense, configuration is the compilation of settings that instruct each device on its function. Each of these components—an IP address, a routing entry, a firewall access list, or a DNS resolver setting—is a piece of configuration. When you consider that this is true of hundreds or thousands of devices, it becomes clear why managing configurations systematically is not just a convenience, but a professional necessity.

Network Configuration Elements

Every device in a network has dozens of configurable elements. For example:

- A router has routing tables, static routes, and dynamic routing protocols.
- A switch has VLAN assignments, spanning tree parameters, and port security rules.
- A firewall has access control lists, NAT mappings, and intrusion detection settings.
- Servers and endpoints hold IP addresses, DNS information, and transport protocol

preferences.

Each of these pieces together form the **configuration state** of the network. If somehow one of it is incorrect, like, misconfigured a default gateway, you will see that suddenly the entire subnet becomes unreachable.

Types of Network Configurations

The configurations can take different forms depending on network design. In **peer-to-peer networks**, each node manages its own configuration without central authority. In **client-server models**, servers define services while clients consume them, requiring different configuration sets. In practice, most modern networks are hybrids, mixing centralized services with distributed control. Each type brings unique challenges: peer-to-peer requires uniform policy enforcement, while client-server requires managing dependencies. This is where automation and programmatic control become indispensable, and this is where C++ enters the picture.

The C++ has always been a language of control and efficiency. Its networking capabilities allow you to work at the level of sockets and protocols, while its libraries expand those capabilities into automation and system orchestration. With **Boost.Asio**, you can manage asynchronous configuration tasks across many devices. With libraries like **libssh**, you can authenticate into remote systems and push configuration changes programmatically. Using **libxml2**, you can interact with XML-based protocols like NETCONF. Overall, the advantage is precision and performance. When you need to roll out configuration changes to hundreds of routers at once, C++ allows you to craft scalable programs that handle connections in parallel, validate responses, and log results for auditing. Instead of relying on manual CLI commands, you gain a reproducible system that enforces configuration policies consistently.

Configuration Quickview

To understand better, you can simply consider a configuration snapshot of a simple router as shown below:

```
interface GigabitEthernet0/1
  ip address 192.168.1.1 255.255.255.0
  no shutdown
ip route 0.0.0.0 0.0.0.0 10.0.0.1
access-list 100 deny tcp any any eq 23
access-list 100 permit ip any any
```

Here, it configures an interface, sets a default route, and applies an ACL blocking Telnet but permitting other traffic. Each line is a configuration directive. If an administrator mistakenly changes **`eq 23`** (Telnet) to **`eq 22`** (SSH), they would block secure management access instead of insecure Telnet. This small misconfiguration could lock out legitimate administrators.

This whole chapter will expand on these foundations by exploring how configurations can be automated, monitored, and secured through C++.

Automating Network Configuration with NETCONF

With the growth in size and complexity of the networks, the management of device configurations, and that too manually, becomes nearly impossible. The logging into each router or switch, typing commands into the CLI, and hoping no mistakes are made is fragile and slow. This is why **NETCONF (Network Configuration Protocol)** was introduced. NETCONF provides a standardized way to **install, edit, and delete configurations** across network devices programmatically. Instead of relying on proprietary command syntaxes, NETCONF uses structured messages, enabling automation, consistency, and easier integration with software tools. The NETCONF was standardized by the IETF (RFC 6241) and is now supported by most enterprise-grade vendors such as Cisco, Juniper, and Huawei. It uses **XML** as its data format, **RPCs (Remote Procedure Calls)** as its communication model, and typically runs over **SSH** for security.

Working of NETCONF

The functioning of NETCONF can be broken down into several building blocks:

1. **Transport Layer**

   The NETCONF operates primarily over SSH, ensuring confidentiality, integrity, and authentication. Once a secure session is established, NETCONF messages can be exchanged.

2. **RPC Layer**

   The client sends requests (called RPCs) to the server (the device), asking for operations like "retrieve configuration," "edit configuration," or "lock datastore." Each RPC is wrapped in XML and uniquely identified.

3. **Operations Layer**

   The NETCONF defines a set of standard operations, including:

   - **<get-config>** – Retrieve configuration from a datastore.
   - **<edit-config>** – Modify configuration data.
   - **<copy-config>** – Replace configuration with another.
   - **<delete-config>** – Remove a configuration datastore.
   - **<lock>/<unlock>** – Prevent changes while editing.

4. **Content Layer**

The actual configuration data is encoded in XML. For example, an interface configuration may appear as an XML tree, where each element corresponds to a setting.

A NETCONF Exchange

Let us consider that we want to retrieve an interface configuration. So here, the client might send:

```
<rpc message-id="101"
xmlns="urn:ietf:params:xml:ns:netconf:base:1.0">
  <get-config>
    <source>
      <running/>
    </source>
    <filter type="subtree">
      <interfaces xmlns="urn:ietf:params:xml:ns:yang:ietf-
interfaces"/>
    </filter>
  </get-config>
</rpc>
```

In response to the client message, the device responds with an XML tree containing the interface configurations.

NETCONF over CLI

As of today, many engineers still rely on CLI scripting to automate configuration, but CLI is **human-oriented**, not machine-oriented. There are different vendors that have different syntaxes, the error handling is inconsistent, and the parsing outputs are also brittle. The NETCONF eliminates these problems by providing **machine-readable XML responses** and a consistent RPC model across vendors.

Also, the C++ can be used to build NETCONF clients that automate tasks such as pulling configurations, validating them, and applying changes. To do this, you will use two main libraries:

- **libssh** for creating secure SSH connections to NETCONF servers.
- **libxml2** for constructing and parsing XML-based NETCONF messages.

This combination allows you to open secure sessions, exchange XML messages, and interpret the structured responses.

Sample Program: NETCONF Client

The following program is a simplified example of a C++ NETCONF client that connects to a device over SSH, sends a **<get-config>** RPC, and prints the response.

```
#include <libssh/libssh.h>
#include <libssh/callbacks.h>
#include <libxml/parser.h>
#include <libxml/tree.h>
#include <iostream>
int main() {
    ssh_session session = ssh_new();
    if (session == nullptr) {
        std::cerr << "Failed to create SSH session" <<
std::endl;
        return -1;
    }
    // Configure session
    ssh_options_set(session, SSH_OPTIONS_HOST, "192.168.1.1");
// device IP
    ssh_options_set(session, SSH_OPTIONS_USER, "admin");
// username
    // Connect
    if (ssh_connect(session) != SSH_OK) {
        std::cerr << "Error connecting: " <<
ssh_get_error(session) << std::endl;
        ssh_free(session);
        return -1;
    }
    // Authenticate
    if (ssh_userauth_password(session, "admin", "password") !=
SSH_AUTH_SUCCESS) {
        std::cerr << "Authentication failed: " <<
ssh_get_error(session) << std::endl;
```

```
        ssh_disconnect(session);
        ssh_free(session);
        return -1;
    }
    // Open NETCONF subsystem
    ssh_channel channel = ssh_channel_new(session);
    ssh_channel_open_session(channel);
    ssh_channel_request_subsystem(channel, "netconf");
    // Send NETCONF <get-config> RPC
    const char* rpc =
        "<rpc message-id=\"101\"
xmlns=\"urn:ietf:params:xml:ns:netconf:base:1.0\">"
        "  <get-config>"
        "    <source><running/></source>"
        "  </get-config>"
        "</rpc>]]>]]>";  // NETCONF requires end-of-message
marker
    ssh_channel_write(channel, rpc, strlen(rpc));
    // Receive response
    char buffer[4096];
    int nbytes = ssh_channel_read(channel, buffer,
sizeof(buffer), 0);
    if (nbytes > 0) {
        buffer[nbytes] = '\0';
        std::cout << "NETCONF Response:\n" << buffer <<
std::endl;
    }
    // Cleanup
    ssh_channel_close(channel);
    ssh_channel_free(channel);
    ssh_disconnect(session);
```

```
    ssh_free(session);
    return 0;
}
```

After this, install **libssh** and **libxml2** as shown below:

```
vcpkg install libssh libxml2
```

Cnext, you then create a Visual Studio project and link against these libraries. You need to replace the IP, username, and password with your device's credentials, and then simply run the program. It will connect via SSH, and will request the running configuration, and then will display the XML response.

This above small client demonstrates how NETCONF really transforms configuration management. This makes possible to do looping through hundreds of devices in parallel. And, in additon, it automatically rolls back misconfigurations by restoring the previous XML states.

Various Network Configuration Tasks

So far, we have learned that the NCM is not just about protocols or building clients to fetch settings. In day-to-day administration, you will constantly face routine tasks that directly affect performance, availability, and security. Some are small, like adjusting TCP socket parameters, while others involve large-scale updates such as changing routing tables or enforcing firewall rules. Each task has its own risks if performed manually, which is why automating them through code is highly valuable.

Common Network Configuration Tasks

1. **Adjusting TCP/UDP Parameters**

You can fine-tune network stacks to adjust socket buffers, retransmission timers, and connection limits. These adjustments directly impact throughput and latency.

2. **Access Control List Management**

The administrator must ensure that access rules are correct and consistently applied across devices. A misconfigured ACL can either block legitimate traffic or expose services.

3. **NAT Configuration**

It is common for enterprise networks to translate addresses between private and public spaces. The availability of services is maintained when NAT rule verification is automated.

4. **Diagnostic Configuration**

The enabling or disabling of logging, SNMP, or telemetry for troubleshooting is a routine task. The automation of these actions guarantees uniformity across various environments.

Sample Program: Adjusting TCP Parameters

Let us say that we need to set the **SO_SNDBUF** and **SO_RCVBUF** options on a socket to tune performance. So here, we can use Winsock2 calls as shown in the following script:

```
#include <winsock2.h>

#include <ws2tcpip.h>

#include <iostream>

#pragma comment(lib, "ws2_32.lib")

int main() {

    WSADATA wsaData;

    WSAStartup(MAKEWORD(2, 2), &wsaData);

    SOCKET sock = socket(AF_INET, SOCK_STREAM, IPPROTO_TCP);

    if (sock == INVALID_SOCKET) {

        std::cerr << "Socket creation failed." << std::endl;

        return 1;

    }

    int sendBuf = 65536; // 64 KB

    int recvBuf = 65536; // 64 KB

    if (setsockopt(sock, SOL_SOCKET, SO_SNDBUF,
(char*)&sendBuf, sizeof(sendBuf)) == SOCKET_ERROR) {

        std::cerr << "Failed to set send buffer." <<
std::endl;

    }

    if (setsockopt(sock, SOL_SOCKET, SO_RCVBUF,
(char*)&recvBuf, sizeof(recvBuf)) == SOCKET_ERROR) {

        std::cerr << "Failed to set receive buffer." <<
std::endl;

    }

    std::cout << "TCP buffers adjusted successfully!" <<
std::endl;

    closesocket(sock);

    WSACleanup();
```

```
    return 0;
}
```

The above is just a small script but it represents the type of low-level configuration task that C++ allows you to automate. It does fine-tune of the sockets for specific workloads like file transfers or streaming. When you are managing hundreds of servers or devices, repeating these tasks manually is not only slow but also error-prone. By writing C++ programs, you build **repeatability and auditability** into every change. If a buffer adjustment works well on one server, you can replicate it across all servers consistently.

Automating Firmware Updates

A network device is only as secure and stable as the software it runs. Vendors regularly release firmware updates to patch vulnerabilities, fix bugs, and improve performance. But updating firmware is one of the riskiest operations: if it fails midway, the device may become unusable. The automation of the firmware updates reduces the chance of error while ensuring all devices stay current with vendor recommendations.

How Automation Helps?

Traditionally, an administrator would log into each device, upload the firmware image, reboot, and hope the process succeeded. This works for a few devices, but not for hundreds spread across multiple sites. Manual methods risk inconsistencies, forgotten devices, or human error.

The automation of the firmware updates lets you:

- **Upload firmware images programmatically** over secure channels.
- **Verify checksum integrity** before applying updates.
- **Schedule reboots** in a controlled manner.
- **Log outcomes** for auditing and rollback.

Sample Program: Uploading Firmware File using SFTP

So here, we can combine **libssh** and C++ to securely transfer a firmware file to a device.

```
#include <libssh/libssh.h>
#include <libssh/sftp.h>
#include <iostream>
#include <fstream>
int main() {
```

```
    ssh_session session = ssh_new();
    ssh_options_set(session, SSH_OPTIONS_HOST,
"192.168.1.10");
    ssh_options_set(session, SSH_OPTIONS_USER, "admin");
    if (ssh_connect(session) != SSH_OK) {
        std::cerr << "Connection failed: " <<
ssh_get_error(session) << std::endl;
        return -1;
    }
    if (ssh_userauth_password(session, "admin", "password") !=
SSH_AUTH_SUCCESS) {
        std::cerr << "Auth failed: " << ssh_get_error(session)
<< std::endl;
        return -1;
    }
    sftp_session sftp = sftp_new(session);
    sftp_init(sftp);
    std::ifstream firmware("firmware.bin", std::ios::binary);
    if (!firmware) {
        std::cerr << "Firmware file not found." << std::endl;
        return -1;
    }
    sftp_file file = sftp_open(sftp, "/tmp/firmware.bin",
O_WRONLY | O_CREAT | O_TRUNC, S_IRWXU);
    char buffer[4096];
    while (firmware.read(buffer, sizeof(buffer)) ||
firmware.gcount() > 0) {
        sftp_write(file, buffer, firmware.gcount());
    }
    sftp_close(file);
    sftp_free(sftp);
```

```
    ssh_disconnect(session);
    ssh_free(session);
    std::cout << "Firmware uploaded successfully." <<
std::endl;
    return 0;
}
```

This above program securely transfers a firmware file to a target device. Once uploaded, you would typically send a NETCONF or vendor-specific RPC to trigger the firmware upgrade and reboot. The firmware updates are one of the most frequent sources of downtime when done incorrectly. In large enterprises, automating firmware updates is a must-have, not a luxury.

Manipulate TCP and UDP Settings

When you create a socket, the operating system quietly applies defaults that are designed for general-purpose traffic, and these defaults are rarely optimized for demanding workloads such as real-time communications or high-throughput data streams. So, if we adjust these TCP and UDP settings programmatically, it may give us the ability to fine-tune latency, reliability, and performance according to the needs of our app.

In TCP, leaving Nagle's algorithm enabled is acceptable for bulk transfers but disastrous for latency-sensitive systems such as online gaming or live trading. By disabling it, you force packets to be sent immediately. Similarly, enabling keepalive probes helps detect dead connections quickly, avoiding long waits for timeouts. For UDP, settings such as increasing buffer sizes or enabling broadcast are essential for supporting video streaming or service discovery within a subnet.

Manipulating TCP

The program below practically guides you to disable Nagle's algorithm, enable keepalives, and resize buffers in C++.

```
#include <winsock2.h>
#include <ws2tcpip.h>
#include <iostream>
#pragma comment(lib, "ws2_32.lib")
int main() {
    WSADATA wsa;
    WSAStartup(MAKEWORD(2,2), &wsa);
```

```
    SOCKET sock = socket(AF_INET, SOCK_STREAM, IPPROTO_TCP);
    int flag = 1;
    setsockopt(sock, IPPROTO_TCP, TCP_NODELAY, (char*)&flag,
sizeof(flag));
    int keepalive = 1;
    setsockopt(sock, SOL_SOCKET, SO_KEEPALIVE,
(char*)&keepalive, sizeof(keepalive));
    int bufSize = 131072;
    setsockopt(sock, SOL_SOCKET, SO_SNDBUF, (char*)&bufSize,
sizeof(bufSize));
    setsockopt(sock, SOL_SOCKET, SO_RCVBUF, (char*)&bufSize,
sizeof(bufSize));
    std::cout << "TCP socket tuned successfully." <<
std::endl;
    closesocket(sock);
    WSACleanup();
}
```

After you run the above script, you will see how quickly socket behavior changes from default to tailored.

Manipulating UDP

Now that you know, enabling broadcast while having UDP allows the datagrams to reach every host on a subnet.

Following is the sample script:

```
#include <winsock2.h>
#include <ws2tcpip.h>
#include <iostream>
#pragma comment(lib, "ws2_32.lib")
int main() {
    WSADATA wsa;
    WSAStartup(MAKEWORD(2,2), &wsa);
    SOCKET sock = socket(AF_INET, SOCK_DGRAM, IPPROTO_UDP);
```

```
    int broadcast = 1;
    setsockopt(sock, SOL_SOCKET, SO_BROADCAST,
(char*)&broadcast, sizeof(broadcast));
    sockaddr_in addr{};
    addr.sin_family = AF_INET;
    addr.sin_port = htons(9999);
    addr.sin_addr.s_addr = INADDR_BROADCAST;
    const char* msg = "UDP broadcast test";
    sendto(sock, msg, strlen(msg), 0, (sockaddr*)&addr,
sizeof(addr));
    std::cout << "UDP broadcast sent!" << std::endl;
    closesocket(sock);
    WSACleanup();
}
```

In the above, the defaults are built for the average workload. This teaches us to engineer networks for the specific demands of our environment, whether that means lightning-fast small packets, robust keepalive detection, or optimized streaming.

Failure Recovery

All administrators make mistakes, and even the most reliable devices can malfunction. For example, a typo in an access control list could lock out administrators, a firmware update could leave a device unstable, and a corrupted configuration could cause routing failures. The question is not if these failures will occur, but when. The goal of recovery is to reduce downtime from hours to minutes.

Building a Recovery Strategy

Now you must know that the recovery always begins with **backups of known good states**. Every configuration change should be preceded by storing the current state in a secure location. Automated rollback should be in place so that if a new configuration renders the device unreachable, the system reverts to its last working state. Some enterprise devices even maintain dual firmware images to provide instant fallback when an update fails.

Restoring Configuration

The program below demonstrates how a configuration file can be restored using **`libssh`** and

SFTP.

```
#include <libssh/libssh.h>
#include <libssh/sftp.h>
#include <iostream>
#include <fstream>
int main() {
    ssh_session session = ssh_new();
    ssh_options_set(session, SSH_OPTIONS_HOST, "192.168.1.1");
    ssh_options_set(session, SSH_OPTIONS_USER, "admin");
    ssh_connect(session);
    ssh_userauth_password(session, "admin", "password");
    sftp_session sftp = sftp_new(session);
    sftp_init(sftp);
    std::ifstream backup("backup_config.txt",
std::ios::binary);
    sftp_file file = sftp_open(sftp, "/tmp/config.txt",
O_WRONLY | O_CREAT | O_TRUNC, S_IRWXU);
    char buffer[4096];
    while (backup.read(buffer, sizeof(buffer)) ||
backup.gcount() > 0) {
        sftp_write(file, buffer, backup.gcount());
    }
    sftp_close(file);
    sftp_free(sftp);
    ssh_disconnect(session);
    ssh_free(session);
    std::cout << "Configuration restored successfully." <<
std::endl;
}
```

This above program restores a backup configuration from a local file to the device, ready to be applied. In your routine practice, you would extend it with error handling and post-restore commands to reload the configuration automatically.

Configure ACL and Firewall

ACL

If configuration is the blueprint of the network, then ACLs (Access Control Lists) and firewalls are the locks and gates. They determine which traffic is allowed and which is blocked. A misconfigured ACL can either block legitimate traffic or leave the door open for attackers. Firewalls extend this concept, offering deeper inspection and stateful filtering. Configuring these elements programmatically ensures consistency and accuracy across the entire infrastructure.

An ACL is simply a set of rules applied to interfaces. Each rule matches packet attributes such as source IP, destination IP, or protocol, and either permits or denies the traffic. ACLs are evaluated in order, with the first match determining the action. This sequential evaluation makes precision critical: a misplaced deny rule can shut down access entirely.

Firewall

Firewalls take packet filtering further by adding **state awareness**. A firewall knows that a packet arriving on port 443 is part of an existing HTTPS session rather than a new request. It can also detect anomalies like malformed packets or traffic surges. Modern firewalls often provide application-level filtering, intrusion prevention, and logging.

With NETCONF or vendor APIs, you can push ACL and firewall rules to devices programmatically. This avoids manual CLI sessions and ensures that every device applies the same policy. C++ acts as the glue between policy definition and device enforcement.

Applying ACL Rule

Following is a simple example of sending a NETCONF **`edit-config`** RPC using **`libssh`** to add a deny rule for Telnet traffic.

```
#include <libssh/libssh.h>
#include <iostream>
#include <string>
int main() {
    ssh_session session = ssh_new();
    ssh_options_set(session, SSH_OPTIONS_HOST, "192.168.1.1");
    ssh_options_set(session, SSH_OPTIONS_USER, "admin");
```

```
    ssh_connect(session);
    ssh_userauth_password(session, "admin", "password");
    ssh_channel channel = ssh_channel_new(session);
    ssh_channel_open_session(channel);
    ssh_channel_request_subsystem(channel, "netconf");
    std::string rpc =
        "<rpc message-id=\"102\"
xmlns=\"urn:ietf:params:xml:ns:netconf:base:1.0\">"
        "  <edit-config>"
        "    <target><running/></target>"
        "    <config>"
        "      <acl xmlns=\"urn:ietf:params:xml:ns:yang:ietf-
acl\">"
        "        <acl-entries>"
        "          <ace>"
        "            <rule-name>deny-telnet</rule-name>"
        "            <matches>"
        "              <protocol>6</protocol>" // TCP
        "              <destination-port>23</destination-
port>"
        "            </matches>"
        "            <actions>"
        "              <forwarding>drop</forwarding>"
        "            </actions>"
        "          </ace>"
        "        </acl-entries>"
        "      </acl>"
        "    </config>"
        "  </edit-config>"
        "</rpc>]]>]]>";
```

```
    ssh_channel_write(channel, rpc.c_str(), rpc.size());
    char buffer[4096];
    int nbytes = ssh_channel_read(channel, buffer,
sizeof(buffer), 0);
    if (nbytes > 0) {
        buffer[nbytes] = '\0';
        std::cout << "Response:\n" << buffer << std::endl;
    }
    ssh_channel_close(channel);
    ssh_channel_free(channel);
    ssh_disconnect(session);
    ssh_free(session);
}
```

This above example adds a deny rule for Telnet (port 23). In practice, you would wrap this logic into reusable functions and push policies across multiple devices simultaneously.

So here, rather than waiting for administrators to manually apply rules, you can instantly enforce global policies. You can also validate configurations against a baseline before deployment to ensure there are no gaps in protection. In industries such as finance and healthcare, where compliance is strict, this automation means the difference between passing and failing audits.

Summary

In summary, you learned that configurations form the invisible backbone of networks, and that managing them systematically is essential to reliability and security. First, you learned how configuration states are distributed across routers, switches, firewalls, and servers. Then, you learned how configuration management prevents errors from spiraling into outages. Then, you explored NETCONF, the standardized protocol for programmatic configuration. You learned how NETCONF operates with RPCs and XML and how to implement a basic client in C++ that retrieves and applies configurations.

Next, you moved on to real-world tasks, such as adjusting TCP and UDP socket parameters, managing access control lists, pushing firewall rules, and automating firmware updates with safety mechanisms. You also learned how to run diagnostic tools continuously with automation, eliminating dependence on manual intervention. You also learned how recovery strategies based on backups and automated rollback can protect networks when failures occur.

Chapter 10: Network Monitoring

Chapter Overview

In this chapter, you will learn how monitoring gives you continuous visibility into the health, performance, and security of your network. You will begin by exploring the concept of network monitoring as the process of collecting, analyzing, and alerting on data from devices and links, and you will see how tools such as Nagios act as a foundation for monitoring hosts and services. You will then focus on fault monitoring, where you will configure checks that immediately detect when devices or services fail and integrate them into a central dashboard. From there, you will move into performance monitoring, where you will track latency, packet loss, jitter, and bandwidth utilization, ensuring that quality of service standards are maintained.

Next, the security monitoring will then take center stage, where you will learn how to detect unauthorized access attempts, policy violations, and anomalous network activity using log checks and port scans. Each section will not only explain the concepts but also include step-by-step demonstrations, showing you how to install Nagios, configure plugins, and even extend its functionality with C++ programs. Overall, the aim of this chapter is to make you understand how to shift from reactive firefighting to proactive oversight, and thereby able to build a monitoring framework that anticipates problems and keeps your network reliable and secure.

Network Monitoring Overview

A network, no matter how carefully designed or robustly deployed, cannot be left unattended. The devices degrade, links fluctuate, services crash, and new threats constantly emerge. Without visibility into what is happening at any given moment, you are flying blind. Network monitoring provides that visibility. It is the continuous process of observing the health, availability, performance, and security of your network to ensure it delivers the expected services to users.

So here, the monitoring is not just about spotting outages. It is about identifying early warnings, understanding trends, and preventing small anomalies from turning into large-scale disruptions. For example, rising CPU usage on a router might indicate an impending failure, while a sudden increase in latency might reveal congestion before users notice slowdowns. If we continue to collect and analyze the metrics, it helps to achieve strong monitoring and thereby it helps you move from reactive firefighting to proactive management.

Core Dimensions of Network Monitoring

The monitoring as a concept intends to covers multiple interdependent areas, including:

- **Fault Monitoring** deals with detecting outright failures, such as a device going down, a service becoming unreachable, or a link dropping.
- **Performance Monitoring** looks at metrics like bandwidth usage, latency, jitter, and packet loss, ensuring that quality of service commitments are met.

- **Security Monitoring** focuses on unauthorized access attempts, anomalies in traffic patterns, or violations of firewall and ACL rules.
- **Account Monitoring** tracks user activity, login attempts, and privilege escalations, which are critical in environments where compliance is important.

And, each of these dimensions requires specialized tools and methods, but they all tie together into one central goal: keeping the network both healthy and secure.

How Monitoring Systems Operate?

A monitoring system has several components. At its heart lies the **collector**, which gathers data from network devices. This data can be retrieved through SNMP queries, log collection, packet sniffing, or API calls. The next component is the **analyzer**, which interprets the collected data, compares it against thresholds, and detects patterns. Then comes the **notifier**, which raises alerts when anomalies or failures are detected. Finally, the **dashboard** provides a visualization of the network state, showing administrators at a glance where attention is needed.

This pipeline makes monitoring not just a passive observer but an active management tool. When a threshold is crossed, say, 80% bandwidth utilization, an alert is triggered. When a host stops responding to pings, the system flags it as down and can even initiate automated recovery scripts.

Why Nagios is Important for Learning

The market for monitoring tools is vast, but a few platforms stand out because of their maturity and adoption. They are as below:

- **Nagios** is one of the most widely used open-source monitoring solutions. It provides host and service checks, threshold-based alerts, and a flexible plugin system that lets administrators monitor almost anything. Its extensibility has made it a standard in many enterprises.
- **Zabbix** offers a more modern architecture with built-in visualization and distributed monitoring capabilities.
- **Prometheus** is popular in cloud-native environments, especially for time-series metrics and integration with Grafana.
- **PRTG** is known for ease of setup and all-in-one monitoring.

Among these, Nagios holds a special place because it pioneered open-source monitoring and remains a solid foundation for building customized monitoring solutions. Many professionals first encounter monitoring through Nagios before extending into other platforms. The Nagios operates on a simple but powerful idea: **everything can be checked**. A host can be pinged, a port can be tested, a log file can be scanned, or a custom script can be executed. The result of that check is then compared against thresholds. If the output is within limits, the service is considered "OK." If not, it is marked "Warning" or "Critical." These results feed into the dashboard and alerts system, keeping administrators informed.

What makes Nagios particularly valuable is its **plugin model**. A plugin is nothing more than a small program that returns a status code and some text. By following this standard, you can monitor not only built-in services but also any custom application you build. If you have a proprietary server listening on port 5050, you can write a C++ program that connects to it, validates the handshake, and returns a status. Nagios will treat it the same as monitoring HTTP or ping.

Fault Monitoring

Coming to fault monitoring, it primarily deals with identifying and reporting problems in the network before they become catastrophic. Imagine a branch router going offline in the middle of the night. If you rely only on users to notice the next morning, your company could lose hours of productivity. If we have the automated fault monitoring in place, the moment the router goes down, the system marks it as unreachable and sends an alert to the administrator, allowing intervention before users are even aware.

The faults are identified by tracking metrics such as packet loss, link status, service availability, and response times. A simple ping failure may indicate a host is unreachable. A sudden increase in response time might mean the service is overloaded. Nagios captures these conditions using **plugins**, each designed to check one type of service or metric. These plugins run periodically, and their results are compared against thresholds. If a threshold is crossed, Nagios generates a warning or critical alert.

Configuring Nagios

Because Nagios runs natively on Linux, the most seamless way to introduce it into a Windows environment is by using **WSL**. Once we have the WSL, we can then run the Nagios side by side with our Windows tools.

To begin with, we first enable WSL and install Ubuntu from the Microsoft Store.

After this, we then update the packages inside Ubuntu:

```
sudo apt-get update && sudo apt-get upgrade -y
```

next, we then install the prerequisites for Nagios:

```
sudo apt-get install build-essential libgd-dev openssl libssl-
dev unzip apache2 php libapache2-mod-php libperl-dev libltdl-
dev wget -y
```

Then, we download and compile Nagios Core:

```
cd /tmp
```

```
wget
https://github.com/NagiosEnterprises/nagioscore/releases/downl
oad/nagios-4.4.6/nagios-4.4.6.tar.gz
tar xzf nagios-4.4.6.tar.gz
cd nagios-4.4.6
./configure --with-httpd-conf=/etc/apache2/sites-enabled
make all
sudo make install
sudo make install-init
sudo make install-config
sudo make install-commandmode
```

After this, we then install and configure the web interface, create an admin user, and start the Nagios service. Once Nagios is running, you access its dashboard at **http://localhost/nagios** from your browser in Windows.

Configuring Fault Monitoring

After installation of the Nagios, we then create the definitions for hosts and services. Like for example, suppose we want to monitor a server at **192.168.1.50**. So here, in our Nagios configuration, we program the following:

```
define host {
    use                linux-server
    host_name          my-server
    address            192.168.1.50
}
define service {
    use                    generic-service
    host_name              my-server
    service_description PING
    check_command          check_ping!100.0,20%!500.0,60%
}
```

This configuration will instruct Nagios to ping the server at regular intervals. If packet loss exceeds 20% or latency exceeds 500 ms, Nagios will generate an alert.

Once active, the Nagios displays host and service statuses in its web interface. You will see your server marked as "UP" when reachable, or "DOWN" when ping fails. The services can show states like "OK," "Warning," or "Critical," depending on thresholds. The faults are also logged, giving you history for troubleshooting.

You can go beyond standard plugins by writing your own in C++. For example, you might write a small program that connects to a TCP port to check if a proprietary service is running. By returning exit codes that follow Nagios plugin standards (0 for OK, 1 for Warning, 2 for Critical), your program integrates seamlessly into Nagios. This duo of conceptual clarity and practical implementation ensures that fault monitoring is not just theoretical, rather you can see it in action: from detecting simple host failures to integrating custom fault detectors written in C++.

Performance Monitoring

A network that is technically "up" can still be unusable if it is performing poorly. Simply you may consider a situation of a corporate video conference where every participant remains connected but speech arrives garbled due to jitter, or a web application where page loads take several seconds because of congestion. From the user's perspective, the network is broken, even if no device has failed. Performance monitoring ensures that the quality of service is tracked continuously, so administrators can fix degradation before it impacts productivity.

Key Performance Parameters

Performance monitoring revolves around a set of measurable parameters. **Latency** measures the time it takes for a packet to travel from source to destination. **Jitter** represents the variation in latency, which is critical in voice and video streams. **Packet loss** shows how many packets fail to reach their destination, directly degrading throughput and reliability. **Bandwidth utilization** tells you how much of the available link capacity is in use. Together, these metrics define whether the network is delivering the experience it was designed for.

Nagios monitors performance through its plugin system. Plugins like **`check_ping`** provide latency and packet loss data. Others, such as **`check_snmp`**, query devices for interface statistics such as input and output octets, which can be used to calculate bandwidth utilization. The results are displayed in the Nagios dashboard with thresholds defined by the administrator. For example, you might set a warning threshold at 70% bandwidth utilization and a critical threshold at 90%.

Monitoring Bandwidth Utilization

Suppose you want to monitor the utilization of a switch port using SNMP. First, you configure the switch to allow SNMP queries. Then, in Nagios, you define a service like this:

```
define service {
    use                              generic-service
```

```
    host_name                   switch1
    service_description         Port_1_Bandwidth
    check_command               check_snmp!-C public -o IF-
MIB::ifInOctets.1 -w 70000000 -c 90000000
}
```

This will instruct the Nagios to query the first port's incoming octets, with thresholds for warning and critical alerts. You can further add a similar check for outgoing octets.

If you want more control, you can build custom performance monitors in C++. For example, you might measure jitter by sending a series of UDP packets and calculating variance in response times. A small program can do this by recording timestamps before sending and after receiving. When integrated as a Nagios plugin, it can alert you if jitter exceeds acceptable levels, such as 30 ms in a VoIP environment.

Security Monitoring

Every network is under constant threat. Attackers probe open ports, malware spreads through unpatched devices, and insiders may attempt to bypass policies. Security monitoring is the process of continuously analyzing network activity to detect and respond to suspicious behavior. Unlike fault or performance monitoring, which track availability and quality, security monitoring focuses on integrity and protection.

Core Security Parameters

At the most basic level, security monitoring involves **unauthorized access attempts**, such as repeated failed login attempts or logins from unusual locations. It also tracks **traffic anomalies**, such as sudden spikes in outbound data that may indicate data exfiltration. Another key area is **policy compliance**, ensuring that firewall rules, ACLs, and encryption standards are applied consistently.

The Nagios was not designed as a full intrusion detection system, but it can act as the first layer of defense. By using plugins, Nagios can check logs for patterns, monitor port states, and verify that firewalls are configured correctly. For example, you can use the **`check_log`** plugin to scan authentication logs for repeated failures, or the **`check_tcp`** plugin to confirm that only intended services are accessible.

Monitoring Login Attempts

Now here, let us assume that you want to monitor SSH login attempts on a Linux host. You could simply define a service in Nagios like this:

```
define service {
```

```
    use                         generic-service
    host_name                   server1
    service_description         SSH_Login_Attempts
    check_command               check_log!/var/log/auth.log!Failed
password
}
```

This will tell the Nagios to scan the authentication log for occurrences of "Failed password." If the count rises above thresholds, Nagios marks the service as critical and triggers an alert.

Extending Security Monitoring

The C++ lets you go beyond predefined checks. For example, you can write a program that listens for unusual port activity. Suppose you expect only ports 22 and 443 to be open on a server. A C++ plugin could periodically scan the server and report any unexpected ports. If the program finds port 21 (FTP) open, it returns a "Critical" status to Nagios, signaling a possible misconfiguration or compromise.

```
#include <winsock2.h>
#include <ws2tcpip.h>
#include <iostream>
#pragma comment(lib, "ws2_32.lib")
int main() {
    const char* host = "192.168.1.20";
    int ports[] = {22, 443};
    bool unexpectedFound = false;
    for (int port = 1; port <= 1024; ++port) {
        SOCKET sock = socket(AF_INET, SOCK_STREAM,
IPPROTO_TCP);
        sockaddr_in addr{};
        addr.sin_family = AF_INET;
        addr.sin_port = htons(port);
        inet_pton(AF_INET, host, &addr.sin_addr);
        if (connect(sock, (sockaddr*)&addr, sizeof(addr)) ==
0) {
```

```
            bool allowed = false;
            for (int expected : ports) if (port == expected)
allowed = true;
            if (!allowed) {
                std::cout << "Unexpected port open: " << port
<< std::endl;
                unexpectedFound = true;
            }
        }
        closesocket(sock);
    }
    return unexpectedFound ? 2 : 0; // 2 = Critical, 0 = OK
}
```

If we compile it as a simply plugin, this program then integrates seamlessly with Nagios to flag unexpected ports. By continuously checking logs, ports, and compliance with policies, you reduce the window of opportunity for attackers. Combined with other dedicated security systems, the Nagios provides a flexible, lightweight way to enforce the security posture of your network, while C++ extends its reach into customized checks for your environment.

Summary

To sum up, you learned that network monitoring was not just about knowing whether a device was alive. It was also about ensuring that the network delivered reliable, secure, and high-quality service to its users. You explored the broad scope of monitoring, beginning with fault monitoring, where you discovered how systems like Nagios could detect outages, service failures, and link problems through automated checks and threshold alerts You then moved on to performance monitoring, where you examined metrics like latency, jitter, packet loss, and bandwidth utilization. In this role, you saw how Nagios plugins and custom C++ programs could make these values visible in real time. Next, you addressed security monitoring, learning how log scanning, port checks, and compliance validation could identify unauthorized activity or misconfigurations before they turned into intrusions. You were also introduced to the Nagios plugin model and learned how C++ could be used to extend its capabilities with custom checks tailored to your environment. By the end of the chapter, you had built a comprehensive picture of monitoring as a proactive discipline. This discipline combined open-source tools, programmable checks, and systematic oversight. It transformed raw data into meaningful, actionable visibility of the entire network.

Index

Epilogue

As I reach the last couple pages of this second edition, I find myself reflecting on the material, and on the kind of transformation that happens when theory meets consistent practice. The idea of network programming can sometimes make developers nervous. It's a mix of system-level programming, protocols, performance, and security, so it takes both patience and precision. But if you go through each chapter with intention and curiosity, you'll build something way more valuable than just isolated skills — you'll build a structured way of thinking about networks.

At the start of this journey, you learned how C++ naturally aligns with networking through its performance, control, and portability. It's like you built socket-based applications, configured IP networks, and implemented application protocols directly through your code. All that experience gave him the technical skills he needed to take on more operational responsibilities. You then get into the nitty-gritty of what network administrators do every day, like automating configurations with NETCONF, updating devices remotely, tweaking TCP and UDP behavior for different environments, and preparing for failures before they happen.

From there, your attention shifted to observing networks intelligently. Things like monitoring faults, tracking performance, watching for security anomalies, and automating diagnostics are what keep real systems alive. When we integrated Nagios and extended it through C++, we saw how monitoring could move from static dashboards to dynamic, programmable oversight. These are the kinds of practices that set reactive firefighting apart from proactive engineering. None of these chapters were standalone. Each one prepared you for the next, layering skills and understanding in a deliberate sequence. This approach reflects how real expertise grows: not through sudden leaps, but through steady accumulation and application.

There's something else I'd like to acknowledge. This book isn't meant to cover every complex networking scenario. It can't handle enterprise-level edge cases, multi-vendor orchestration, or advanced protocol engineering. Instead, the idea has always been to give you a solid foundation of practical skills and the confidence to build on them. With that foundation, exploring specialized areas becomes way less scary.

If you've made it this far, writing the code, running the examples, setting up the tools, and thinking through the scenarios, then you've already taken big steps toward becoming more than just a C++ developer who knows networking. You're becoming someone who can administer, automate, and troubleshoot real networks with intent. That's a skill set that'll keep on giving. But the real work starts when you put the book down. Whatever you're writing in your scripts, whatever you're automating in your configurations, and whatever systems you're monitoring — every single one of these is a chance to get better at your job.

I encourage you to keep experimenting, keep asking questions, and keep building.

Thank You

www.ingramcontent.com/pod-product-compliance
Lightning Source LLC
Chambersburg PA
CBHW080215170726
48282CB00030B/1131
* 9 7 8 8 1 9 7 4 1 6 5 4 5 *